The Future of Theory

Blackwell Manifestos

In this new series major critics make timely interventions to address important concepts and subjects, including topics as diverse as, for example: Culture, Race, Religion, History, Society, Geography, Literature, Literary Theory, Shakespeare, Cinema, and Modernism. Written accessibly and with verve and spirit, these books follow no uniform prescription but set out to engage and challenge the broadest range of readers, from undergraduates to postgraduates, university teachers and general readers – all those, in short, interested in ongoing debates and controversies in the humanities and social sciences.

The Future of Theory

Jean-Michel Rabaté

Blackwell
Publishers

Editorial Offices:
108 Cowley Road, Oxford OX4 1JF, UK
    Tel: +44 (0)1865 791100
350 Main Street, Malden, MA 02148-5018, USA
    Tel: +1 781 388 8250

First published 2002 by Blackwell Publishers Ltd, a Blackwell Publishing company.

Library of Congress Cataloging-in-Publication Data has been applied for.

ISBN 0-631-23012-2 (hbk) ISBN 0-631-23013-0

A catalogue record for this title is available from the British Library.

Set in 11.5 on 13.5 pt Bembo
by SNP Best-set Typesetter Ltd, Hong Kong
Printed and bound in Great Britain by MPG Books Ltd, Bodmin, Cornwall

For further information on Blackwell Publishers, visit our website:
www.blackwellpublishers.co.uk

149
R

Contents

v

Introduction

Traditionally, philosophy starts with a sense of wonder. Then theory steps in with heavy tread to explain the sources and reasons of the glorious wonder. I will take as my point of departure my own sense of wonder, or rather the sharp jolt I experienced a few years ago as I came across a remark by Judith Butler in an essay originally read at a 1989 conference, "Imitation and Gender Insubordination," and then published in 1991 – all these dates are not indifferent, as we will see. Judith Butler, whom I had always identified with the "cutting edge" of contemporary American theory and admired for her groundbreaking analyses of performative gender, her intense dialogues with philosophy and psychoanalysis, evinced a worried ambivalence facing the very notion of theory:

> I do not understand the notion of "theory," and am hardly interested in being cast as its defender, much less in being sig-nified as part of an elite gay/lesbian theory crowd that seeks to establish the legitimacy and domestication of gay/lesbian studies within the academy. Is there a pregiven distinction between theory, politics, culture, media? How do those divi-sions operate to quell a certain intertextual writing that might well generate wholly different epistemic maps? But I am writing here now: is it too late?[1]

The sense of an extreme urgency, of pressing historical considera-tions, of a brisk calendar whose agendas risk being stale, underpins almost all recent essays on the state of theory, and it should be heard echoing – although in a more ironical way – in my own title for this book.

If one does not want to say just that tomorrow the blind will not see and the deaf will not hear, one can hardly write a book about the "future" without taking stock of past events and inscribing oneself in a historical mode. And as we will see, the peculiar history of Theory, like that of fashion, tends to describe loops and circles; in short, if one takes enough distance, it is possible to see it as rather cyclical. What remains "future" should be contained in the sense of an agency, of agendas, of tasks to prioritize, of dead ends to acknowledge for what they often are, the forced awareness of one's limits. The sense of a similar urgency pervades Butler's self-admonitions: "If the political task is to show that theory is never merely *theoria*, in the sense of disengaged contemplation, and to insist that it is fully political (*phronesis* or even *praxis*), then why not simply call this operation *politics*, or some necessary permutation of it?"[2] If I wish to be true to my half-serious claim to be writing for the future, I will have to sketch a genealogy of that loaded word *theoria*, a genealogy highlighting particularly strong moments of incandescence and dissemination, of confrontation and misunderstandings. If I may anticipate slightly, one of the points I will try to make is that *theoria* has never been "disengaged contemplation," and that even when Theory was depicted at its most ludicrously abstract and oblivious of material contingencies through the famous anecdote of Thales who fell down a well because he was gazing at the stars, one cannot forget that Thales was not only a philosopher and an observer of the heavens, not only the first name who can be credited with a systematic attempt at separating philosophy from myth, but also a statesman with political ambitions. In a very interesting parallel with our times, he clamored for a need to go beyond the limited model of the early nation-state or Greek *polis* and thus suggested the creation of a supranational and totally rational league of Ionic cities. In an early note, Nietzsche drew attention to this apparent contradiction: "*Thales' league of cities*: he saw the fatal destiny of the *polis* and saw that myth was the foundation of the *polis*. If he broke down myth then perhaps he

praxis

2

also broke up the *polis*. Thales as a statesman. The struggle against the *polis*."[3]

Should theory be called politics? Rather than stress the disingenuous nature of such dismissive reduction of theory to absent-minded star-gazing when it comes from a very visible theoretician of gender and sexuality, moreover from a scholar who began her remarkable career by writing an authoritative Ph.D. on the reception of Hegel by major French thinkers like Kojève, Sartre, Lacan, Deleuze, and Foucault[4] – a starting point which has its importance, as I will show in chapter 1 – I wish to meditate on Butler's symptomatic aloofness and wonder whether it signals a new consensus, a spreading reluctance to either "do" or "let do" theory. Even if in the first quote we may assume that theory refers only to "gay/lesbian theory," the assessment fits very well with a pervasive feeling that "theory" has been too one-sided, the mere half (in the best of cases) of a whole in which the missing element is by definition truer, more vital, more essential. Such a radical incompletion would be heightened by an illusion of autonomy generating the monster: not "theories of this or that" but Theory *per se*. I will henceforth capitalize "Theory" when I mean theory in general, leaving the lower case to refer to particular theories.

Whether we call the missing half "praxis" as in the days of Althusserian Marxism, when "Theory" meant the "true" philosophy of dialectical materialism and "praxis" day-to-day militancy (i.e., being busy with tracts, meetings, demonstrations) in a curious continuation of Sartre's Critique of Practical Reason by other means; or whether we call it just "politics," as in the American universities of the 1990s, when the phrase "the politics of –" could apply to everything from high cuisine to low culture, without forgetting Desire, possibly the most pervasive myth of the twentieth century; the problem with Theory seems to be that it is always accused of having missed something. Theory is missing out on "life," real life that is, as in the expression "Get a life!" about "real" sexuality, "real" politics, and so on. Prophetically, Rimbaud had written "True life is elsewhere." This post-Romantic yearning for an unattainable Other construed as more real and more alive has never sounded so true as when dealing with Theory.

One can easily notice a curious paradox today, a paradox which stems from attitudes close to that of Judith Butler's: Theory's demise has been repeatedly announced, the reign of Theory is embalmed in a catalogue of past or post- movements neatly labeled, like those kings or popes who are only remembered by two dates (we can then say that Theory reigned supreme between 1975 and 1991, in the USA at least), yet there have never been so many guides, anthologies, critical readers, symposia, gatherings of new approaches, launchings of methodological recapitulations issued by major academic presses. What Elizabeth Bruss gleefully described in her incisive book *Beautiful Theories* (1982) was the sudden irruption of an "Age of Theory": *"Suddenly, an Age of Theory . . . "* She describes how American universities felt the "invasion" of foreign (mostly French) theoreticians in the early 1970s, how the annual bibliography of the Modern Language Association only listed "aesthetics" and "literary criticism" until 1967, then created a new category called "Literary Criticism and Literary Theory" – a double heading still relevant today – whose listed publications grew from 200 to 600 in 1975, while a spate of new journals (she mentions almost twenty of these) gave regular columns to debates generated by all these new essays, books, conferences. It is a great pity that Elizabeth Bruss died before her own book was published, not only because of the remarkable sensitivity she displays, but also because she would have been an ideal witness to assess what has taken place since then, in the first decade of a new millennium in which Theory has lost its charms; it is not Beautiful any more, but, if not downright ugly yet, a little embarrassing, like a distant cousin full of outdated dreams of grandeur, silly daydreams more adapted to those far away countries in which one still finds students' dorms displaying posters of Mao, Marilyn, or Che Guevara.

Take a recent article published in the *New York Times* about the new buzzword in Theory, which would be "Empire." Emily Eakins's "What Is the Next Big Idea? The Buzz is Growing"[5] begins symptomatically with a recapitulation of these earlier carefree days contrasting strikingly with current anxieties; these anxieties generally stem from the fear of having missed the new wave, whatever it may be. To be sure, the article is not about the publication of a totally new book, but takes stock of a Freudian after-effect when analyzing the emergence to fame of a book published more than a year earlier, in March 2000:

> It comes along only once every decade or so, typically arriv-
> ing without much fanfare. But soon it is everywhere: domi-
> nating conferences, echoing in lecture halls, flooding scholarly
> journals. Every graduate student dreams of being the one to
> think it up: the Next Big Idea.
>
> In the 1960s it was Claude Lévi-Strauss and structuralism.
> In the 1970s and 1980s it was Jacques Derrida and decon-
> struction, Michel Foucault and poststructuralism and Jacques
> Lacan and psychoanalysis, followed by various theorists of
> postcolonialism and New Historicism.
>
> And now scholars are wondering if the latest contender
> for academia's next master theorist is Michael Hardt, a self-
> effacing, 41-year-old associate professor of literature at Duke
> University and the co-author of *Empire*, a heady treatise on
> globalization that is sending frissons of excitement through
> campuses from Sào Paulo to Tokyo. (B7)

If Jameson and Žižek, two main voices among the theoretical opinion-makers, earlier praised the book, announcing it as "the first great new theoretical synthesis of the new millennium" or comparing with Marx's *Communist Manifesto*, Hardt's own opinion is more measured. Refusing the idea that he might be the "next Derrida" (these titles are often conferred upon you by total strangers, as one is chosen to be the next Buddha), he says, alluding to his co-author, Toni Negri:

> Toni and I don't think of this as a very original book. We're
> putting together a variety of things that others have said. That's
> why it's been so well received. It's what people have been
> thinking but not really articulated. (B9)

Such candor is rare, and may betray a rare and reassuring modesty – a previous book by the same authors, Hardt and Negri (the latter was not yet serving a sentence in an Italian jail), *Labor of Dionysus*,[6] had been launched with some fanfare seven years earlier but did not do nearly as well as *Empire*, perhaps because it begins by presenting its conceptual instruments as Theory's Jurassic Park, immediately posing the bland question, when laying on the table from the outset its conceptual starting points (labor, exploitation, class conflict, proletarian struggles, the need to elaborate a Marxist theory of the state): "Do dinosaurs still walk the earth?"[7] This is the point when most hurried graduate students put the book back on its shelf. Moreover, what was lacking from this interesting and original contribution to Marxist scholarship was, precisely, the new buzzword of "globalization" – a term tellingly absent from the index in the 1994 book, but which has become the central issue in *Empire*.

On the other hand, the *New York Times* article was quite timely, appearing just a few days before the Genoa Summit of the eight leading industrialized nations which opened on July 21, 2001 and closed on random arrests, savage beatings, and the haunting image of one young man shot to death, which shattered lots of well-meaning illusions. Accordingly, Negri and Hardt were able to confirm the self-fulfilling prophecy of the article praising their book: they found a tribune in the Op-Ed tribune of the *New York Times* for July 20, not only explaining "What the Protesters in Genoa Want"[8] but also showing that it would be absurd to simply oppose globalization. While *Empire* advocates a very abstract "Revolution" whose contours are strategically blurred, Hardt's and Negri's actual program sounds quite moderate, more in line with the idea of "constituent subjects" with which they concluded *Labor of Dionysus*:

> The protests themselves have become global movements, and one of their clearest objectives is the democratization of globalizing processes. This should not be called an anti-globalization movement. It is pro-globalization, or rather an alternative globalization movement – one that seeks to eliminate inequalities between rich and poor and between the powerful and the powerless, and to expand the possibilities of self-determination.[9]

Where would one find, one might ask, the rabid right-wing Scrooge who would refuse to subscribe to such a generous and universal program?

Let us then try to understand the role played by Theory in this simple example. As the first article quoted explains, what made the popularity of a philosopher like Jacques Derrida such a sudden and modish phenomenon was less due to his ideas than to a certain timeliness in the introduction of a new style of discourse. Michèle Lamont observed in 1987 that Derrida's popularity in American campuses was generated above all by a specific mode of writing, and also by the way he would pose the complex or essential questions to academics at a time when a disciplinary crisis was rampant in the humanities.[10] Lamont refers to Derrida's French accent and stylish clothes – which, although distinctive enough, do not go to the heart of the matter. It is indeed an issue of "style," but here style is the "man itself" as Buffon and Lacan were wont to say; in fact "style" leads to a rethinking of fundamental issues in times of institutional or definitional disarray. Hence, it goes deeper than the superficial layers represented by clothes, no matter how important they are (since, after all, deconstruction is credited with having given birth to a certain fashion in clothes): it touches on the body. By which I do not mean that we should look for hidden tattoos, but that the eruption of fashionable discourses in the academic scene has always been accompanied by the creation of a new corpus. Theory is thus a *Sartor Resartus* in progress, transforming an apparently futile miscellany of transcendental thoughts in a new writing that is at the same time a self-conscious reflection on writing that will "excite us to self-activity" to quote Carlyle's own words.[11]

Just as the rise of Lévi-Strauss in the 1960s opened wide the doors of new linguistic and anthropological libraries, the fame of deconstruction was marked by the fact that every student was forced to discover pell-mell Plato, Levinas, Hegel, Husserl, Heidegger, Bataille, Mallarmé, to name just a few of the authors Derrida made popular overnight. Derrida's success owed thus not a little to the fact that most Anglo-Saxon readers had not been exposed to the kind of history of philosophy that is still taught at high-school level in France and Italy, where most undergraduates will have read a selection of canonical texts by, say, Plato, Aristotle, Descartes, Kant, and Hegel. When he added to this, with a virtuosity that is so characteristic, a number of apparent non-philosophers like Artaud, Mallarmé, Valéry, or Joyce so as to "read" them along the lines of a philosophical investigation probing the function of language, more precisely the repression of rhetoric or "writing," Derrida radicalized and systematized a gesture already performed by Heidegger. Heidegger, it is true, commanded over a much smaller literary corpus, limited essentially to three poets, Hölderlin, Trakl, and Rilke, names which would appeal above all to students of German literature but would lose their appeal for all others, while Derrida not only opened wide the doors to another library but also paved the way to a joyous and seemingly infinite "inmixing" of literary and philosophical texts. It was thus not a coincidence that Derrida and Paul de Man, when they met in 1966, discovered so many affinities: they had both been marked by the reading of Heidegger, Nietzsche, and Blanchot, and were bringing to bear a rhetorical inflexion both to "pure" philosophical problematic and to "pure" literary criticism. On the other hand, Theory is not just philosophy and it should not stray too far from the humanities, by which I mean it has to keep a bond, however flexible and dialectical it may be, with literature. Or Theory *is* literature, if you want, but literature raised to the power of speculation, literature when the term includes the "question of literature" or "the thinking of literature." Some periods have delegated their writers to the front of burning political issues, in such a way that the distinction between philosophy and literature has been blurred. Just think of Dante and the politics of Florence, or of Confucius, whose thwarted political ambitions left him time enough to prepare a famous poetic anthology of Chinese folk-songs.

It is thus not enough to say that Theory should by definition address contemporary issues like globalization, or the various attempts by superpowers to regulate the more and more asthmatic well-being of the inhabitants of the planet. Using different means than demonstrations, fundraising, or lobbying, means that remain closer to the status of a text, Theory functions as a witness in an ongoing trial, and its necessity arises from the moment one realizes that there is precisely such a trial, be it in the field of the humanities or of justice, politics, bioethics, the environment, and so on.

Facing these issues, Theory is supposed to ask difficult, foundational questions that all somehow entail revisionary readings of culture and its foundational texts. While it does not necessarily have any answer, at least it knows where to appeal. My main contention in these pages is that Theory should not be ashamed of its double Greek origins, which point both to a "pure" intellectual contemplation and to ritual witnessing in the framework of the city or policy – as I will show in more detail in a later chapter. This is why Theory is never compromised enough and why Heidegger is one of its favorite authors. Unlike Kant's reason, Theory can never be pure because it is always lacking, and this weakness is in fact its strength. What I see, however, as Theory's main effect in the production of knowledge and the dissemination of discourses can be described as a process of hystericization. As Michael Hardt willingly confessed, the success of *Empire* might be due to its giving people what they already wanted without knowing it exactly. The "buzzword" in this case was true to its name: two weeks after the publication of the article, the book had sold out, the last copies had disappeared from bookstores, and it was then immediately reissued as a paperback.

If Theory plays the trick of the "globalizing" gesture without really being able to define itself, this lack of definition is alone capable of questioning huge monsters like "globalization" and should send us on historical parallels with a similar theoretical fading effect: across the centuries, hysteria could never be adequately defined by medical knowledge as a positive disease with clear symptoms and a detailed nosography. Charcot and Freud after him attempted to surround it with a new theater, from the literal amphitheaters at La Salpêtrière where Charcot exhibited his patients in front of a fashionable crowd, to the more secluded setting in which a bourgeois couch, deep with pillows and carpets, will restrict movements and limit interactions to speech. To illustrate my analogy, rather than reopen the fascinating but labyrinthine volumes of Charcot, Janet, Freud, and Breuer, I choose to return to André Breton's and Louis Aragon's joint manifesto in praise of Hysteria published in *La Révolution surréaliste*, in order to assert, as Lacan declared some forty years later, that hysteria gives birth to a discourse and maintains a quest for truth that always aims at pointing out the inadequacies of official, serious, and "masterful" knowledge.

In the eleventh issue of *La Révolution surréaliste* published in March 1928, Breton and Aragon celebrate the fiftieth anniversary of the invention of hysteria, dated from 1878, an invention which they called "the greatest poetic discovery of the latter part of the century, and we do this at a time when the dismemberment of the concept of hysteria appears to be complete."[12]

Before pursuing the analysis, I would like to offer something that might look slightly forced: let us only replace "hysteria" by "Theory," and then we will produce an adequately updated version of the Surrealists' bold survey. Indeed, if we agree to take as a point of departure the publication of *Writing Degree Zero* by Roland Barthes in 1953 (a starting point which is not wholly arbitrary, as I will try to show in chapter 2), we can easily count half a century till now, that is a time when Theory's death, as we have seen,[13] is often announced prematurely, or heralded as "out" in mainstream academic circles after the heady enthusiasm of the 1970s and 1980s. And yet, like hysteria, Theory never stops coming back, at least under slightly different guises – which is confirmed by the huge number of anthologies, companions, guides, and new introductions. If Theory is reduced to the ghost of itself, then this is a very obtrusive ghost that keeps walking and shaking its chains in our old academic castles. It looks today as if we were assisting in this old paradox: because of Theory's alleged demise, the publication industry and the academic institutions are frantically searching for an answer, a solution, or at least some indication of what the future will be made of. My ambition in this book is to partially answer these legitimate concerns.

To pursue the analogy, let us read to the end the impassioned appeal to poetic and scientific rigor by which Breton and Aragon conclude their manifesto (in which we will have by now replaced "hysteria" with our hypostatized Theory). They have to provide their own counter-definition of a state which has so far eluded medical categorization:

Hysteria [Theory] is a more or less irreducible mental state characterized by a subversion of the relations between the subject and the ethical universe by which the subject feels determined in practice, outside any systematic delirium. This mental state is based on the need for a reciprocal seduction, which explains the hastily accepted miracles of medical suggestion (or counter-suggestion). Hysteria [Theory] is not a pathological phenomenon and can in every respect be considered a supreme vehicle of expression.[14]

The "need for reciprocal seduction" offers a useful key in light of the praise for this "supreme vehicle of expression" in which brute poetry and potential pathology meet. Let us not forget that Breton and Aragon wish to shock their audience, which is why they assert that it was a good thing to see La Salpêtrière's interns regularly sleep with their beautiful hysterical patients because they could not distinguish "between their professional commitment and their taste for love."[15] One can only imagine the scandalous overtones of sexual harassment in our more puritan contexts! In this commendation of hysteria, Breton and Aragon attack their former "master" Babinski, who had taken a view totally opposite to Charcot's by concluding that hysteria did not exist as such and, since it was imaginary or mimetic, would be eradicated if treated by strong suggestion. His harsh treatment of male hysterics during World War I led to medical abuse, including gruesome electrical shock-therapy which was forcefully denounced by the Surrealists.

The parallel with hysteria is relevant because most critics of Theory denounce it either as a fake "Master discourse" referring all extant texts or discourses back to bold or sweeping theses on issues like the invention of homosexuality, the need to bypass Western metaphysics, or the belief that our most secret libidinal dispositions are predetermined by a few bad puns; or as a simply epigonal and sycophantic discourse, the endless reiteration of strategies found in the works of Foucault, Derrida, Lacan, Butler, Žižek, and so on. What is felt to be dangerous is precisely the seduction contained in the mixture of lack of rigor and grandiose pronouncements. Those who most strongly object to the seductive aspects of Theory would then tend to consider it almost as a pathological phenomenon, but whenever they try to denounce what they see as fake mastery and real mimicry, by a logic which pertains more to hysterical contagion than to sedate intellectual debate, they find themselves falling into ranting denunciations. The most notorious example of these vituperations is probably that of Camille Paglia, someone who, I have to admit, managed to introduce a breath of fresh air in the early 1990s, when American excesses of mimetic adulation made me uneasy to be thought of as a disciple of the French master-thinkers. Her favorite mode of address is shooting from the hip in a random spraying of bullets, a drive-by critique which produces some felicities ("Lacan is a Freud T-shirt shrunk down to the teeny-weeny Saussure torso")[16] and too many absurdities ("Heraclitus . . . contains everything that is in Derrida and more";[17] "Lytton Strachey, notably in his treatment of Florence Nightingale as a secret imperialism, has Foucault's debunking method already")[18] to be taken wholly seriously. Besides, how can both Foucault and Derrida be wrong, perverse, and uninformed, if they simply repeat what a few great writers and thinkers of the past have already written?

Yet, Paglia insists upon seriousness, both in her plea for a return to scholarly standards and in her nostalgic glance back to the spirit of the 1960s. Paglia's idols are Mick Jagger, Bob Dylan, and Jimi Hendrix, hip stars unjustly debunked or outflanked by dry French intellectualism! In an involuntary parody of Nietzschean genealogies of academic morals, she depicts Theory as the derisive weapon of the man of resentment betraying a slave-mentality; the revenge of those who do not dare reach to the stars or live spaciously: "The thunderous power chords of hard rock smash the dreary little world of French theory. The French have no sense of elemental realities. They could never have produced a D. H. Lawrence, a Neruda, an Allen Ginsberg."[19] No matter that these three names often turn up positively in Deleuze and Guattari's works like *Thousand Plateaus* – it is undeniable that they are not French. Poetic heroism has dwindled and a race of dwarves has taken over, exploiting as much American stupidity and provincialism as the favorable context, when American universities became aggressive capitalistic corporations in which ideas would follow the ups and downs of a brisk intellectual market:

> The French invasion of the Seventies had nothing to do with leftism or genuine politics but everything to do with good old-fashioned American capitalism, which liberal academics pretend to scorn. The collapse of the job-market, due to reces-

sion and university retrenchment after the baby-boom era, caused economic hysteria. As faculties were cut, commercial self-packaging became a priority. Academics, never renowned for courage, fled beneath the safe umbrella of male authority and one-man rule: the French bigwigs offered to their disciples a soothing esoteric code and a sense of belonging to an elite, an intellectually superior unit, at a time when the market told academics they were useless and dispensable.[20]

It is not that Paglia despairs of Theory – in fact, quite in conformity with her Romantic ideals, she would welcome a stronger Theory, the really big (but impossible) Theory of everything whose disappearance she typically laments. She writes an elegy for the past scholars who did not care for immediate gratification or richly endowed intellectual recognition.

> A scholar's real audience is not yet born. A scholar must build for the future, not the present. The profession is addicted to the present, to contemporary figures, contemporary terminology, contemporary concerns. Authentic theory would mean mastery of the complete history of philosophy and aesthetics. What is absurdly called theory today is just a mask for fashion and greed.[21]

Paglia's hesitation between pure nostalgia (everything was headed in the right direction with the counter-culture of the 1950s until its very excesses killed it) and vague gesturing toward a future control over disinterested knowledge indicates that her aim is to expose the ills of the present in the name of absent values. Despite her tough take-no-prisoners attitude, Paglia obeys the logic of the hystericization effect of Theory as it was perceived early in the 1970s and immediately denounced by its opponents; these would complain about how their students had been seduced and moved away from canonical literature or serious philosophy to mix the two hopelessly. The sense of a deliberate muddle was how deconstruction, for instance, was first received in the United States, which then triggered a heated debate between its own defenders, critics like Rodolphe Gasché wishing to introduce more philosophical dignity while others like Geoffrey Bennington were content to play along in the space between literature and philosophy. Fewer were those who wished to continue playing "freely" in an anarchistic subversion of all frontiers separating genres, which had led to Rorty's tongue-in-cheek praise of the early Derrida as an ironical anti-foundationalist.

In her hystericized response Paglia sends back to Theory its truth as an echo or an inverted message, according to the Lacanian motto, which confirms that Theory is indeed "about" hysteria, a mass hysteria that spreads easily. The only way one can add one's name to the roster is by forcing the Master to admit of his or her impotence (Paglia is as critical of tenured feminists as of their French dancing masters). Even though she professes to like Freud and hate Lacan, she has produced a Lacanian version rather than a Freudian version of hysteria in her wholesale attack on Theory. In fact, Paglia is quite true to the pattern sketched by Lacan's theory of the discourse of the hysteric, especially in connection with scientific discourse. This is quite apparent when she looks for symptoms of the new disease (the spreading of Theory as rampant hysteria on Ivy League campuses): "I will never forget the first time I heard the name "Lacan," pronounced by a fellow woman graduate student at a Yale cocktail party with a haughty, clarion-like, head-tossing, triumphant smugness of discovery that would have embarrassed Marie Curie."[22] The judgment falls without appeal, and its consequences are drastic: "Lacan is a tyrant who must be driven from our shores."[23]

Our tyrant Lacan was working in the 1960s on a fusion between Marx and Freud, not only stating that it was Marx who had "invented the symptom," but also working with economic terms: one could coin a Freudian *Mehrlust* (surplus enjoyment) as a libidinal equivalent of Marx's surplus value (*Mehrwert*). This insight, which brought him rather close to the critical theory of the Frankfurt school, a movement which had remained very far from his main preoccupations, led to the elaboration of the theory of the four discourses which is exposed in the 1969–70 *Seminar*. These discourses are ascribed to four sites of agency rather than four characters; they are the Master, the Hysteric, the Psychoanalyst, and the University. I will focus on the discourse of the Hysteric, noting that this is not a clinical category but a discursive concept or a theoretical construction by which one can interpret and criticize ideological formations. The crisscrossing produced by the discourse of the University, the discourse of the Master, the discourse of the Hysteric, and the discourse of the Analyst[24] accounts for the knotted structure of the social link. Science is associated with the discourse of the Hysteric insofar as it aims at producing new knowledge, while it is linked with the discourse of the University when this knowledge is catalogued and transmitted. In his *Seminar* Lacan repeatedly told the leftist students aiming at "subversion" that, on the one hand, the Maoist models of cultural revolution or collectivist society they admired realized the domination of the discourse of the University, clearly a dream of the Bureaucracy achieving power; and on the other hand, they themselves were in quest of a Master, and sooner or later they would find him.[25] Let me add that he did not see himself in this role, since he pictured himself primarily as an analyst. By an irony equivalent to the reversal of roles I have described with Paglia, who calls up nostalgically a dream of absolute knowledge while hysterically denouncing hysteria, Lacan ended up, in fact, in the unenviable role of a Master for a whole generation.

Freud had posited three main "impossible" but ineluctable professions: to educate, to govern, and to psychoanalyze. Lacan added a fourth task, no less ineluctable: to theorize, that is to "understand" fully by traversing an experience like that of psychoanalysis, then making sense of it by creating powerful concepts that are adequate to the vision, all the while keeping the *libido sciendi* alive, in a desiring dialectic best exemplified by the discourse of the Hysteric.[26] For a psychoanalyst it is crucial to see that the acquisition of knowledge should never be reached at the cost of forgetting subjective and unconscious enjoyment. A discourse appears as the result of the interaction between a divided subject, an always elusive object of desire, and two terms limning the subject's epistemology: S1, or the master-signifier which will replace the lost object, and S2, unconscious knowledge underwriting the pursuit of intellectual interests. The main signifier S1 provides an ideal or a program while connecting knowledge with its dynamic of hidden "surplus enjoyment." These terms make a point which is crucial about Theory as we use it in our scholarship, with the need to find a "master-signifier" as a theme or just a title in a thesis. The master-signifier should not

15

simply mark a territory's difference from all others, but also keep alive some of the initial enjoyment that led to its discovery. Quite often the success of scholarly research will depend upon the horizon of potentialities or the feeling of endless riches generated by a single word chosen as task and field. Knowledge is produced, that is drawn out in some sort of self-education articulating one's libidinal stakes and the unfolding of a chain of words. The discourse of the Hysteric will want to put the subject in the first place, but in order to insist upon subjective division in the quest for the master-signifier. Often one single signifier (for Camille Paglia it is "Theory," condensing the whole phantom of "French theory" and leading to her desire for a better theory) will orient the quest and be taken for the whole truth, perhaps in the hope of proving that all theoreticians are essentially wrong or lacking somewhere.

If Theory reproduces this pattern, it is because it has anticipated it, by what could be described either as a hermeneutical circle or a hysterical ellipsis. Theory will indeed aim at questioning all types of knowledge and discourses by creating an effect of seduction and of bafflement. In doing so, it will generate some kind of knowledge and will aim, no doubt, at a truth. This knowledge will entail certain requirements which will have to remain provisionally in the conditional. First, since it retains a libidinal edge, Theory should not be boring; it should move, seduce, entrance, keep desire in motion, in other words, it should be "sexy". Secondly, Theory cannot be naive and bypass the determination by historical and political contexts: it can found a new discourse only if it remains aware of the previous accumulation of knowledge in the various domains that intersect on its "body." Thirdly, as hysteria fuses with historical modes and fashions in such a way that it is often not visible at all, it fades into the landscape of culture and its various languages. This is why I will need to historicize the movement that has led to the dissemination of the term "Theory" in English-speaking countries. From a broader perspective, one may say that some periods appear to have been more "hystericized" than others: the urgent and constant questioning of values coming from Socrates in classical Athens, the new synthesis brought about by the Schlegel brothers and their friends in a budding German nation, or the impact exerted by a Carlyle on a still young Victorian culture have not found exact equivalents at all times. What they performed in the name of philosophy or critique, by producing hybrid texts, unwritten dialogues, experimental novels, discourses, letters, pamphlets, or pseudo-biographies, had the function I ascribe to Theory: to startle an audience and make it demand new moral, political, or intellectual justifications for what passes as a group's collective values and cultural identity. First of all I will therefore sketch a genealogy of the cultural developments that led to the inauguration of High Theory in the 1960s, with the hope that the knowledge gained may have implications for the future.

This program is necessary because I want to avoid both the eternalizing gesture – Theory would have always existed and would be identified with these mixed genres, with us since Plato, say – and a historicizing contextualization that would present Theory as a succession of "schools" or a panoply of "tools." Having had the dubious honor of being classified in anthologies as a deconstructionist, a Lacanian, a poststructuralist, and a textual geneticist with new historicist leanings, I know how fallible and glib and easy the usual pigeonholings have been in these matters. Besides, having overcome my surprise at being labeled this or that, I would be loath to restrict Theory to a slightly more philosophical version of "literary theory" or "aesthetics." Theory defines a broad site upon which four main domains enmesh and interact: philosophy, history, sciences like linguistics and psychology, and literature (often with the help of the fine arts). The interplay between these overlapping circles creates waves of power and ripples of knowledge that are often hard to differentiate, as Foucault had noted. They plead for the current use of a global Theory as opposed to "theory of . . ." These interlocking domains nevertheless become active only for certain agents engaged in various practices, be they either Althusser's notion of a theoretical practice aiming at the production of knowledge, or more simply the everyday task of teaching literature. I guess that most of us would agree that there is no teaching without some sort of mutual seduction, which will ultimately set in motion our most basic ethical questions, to call up once more the terms used by Breton and Aragon.

This libidinal drifting also explains why hysteria leads to science. In his 1973 televised lecture simply entitled *Television*, Lacan all but identified the discourse of science with the discourse of hysteria:

17

I conclude that scientific discourse and the hysteric's discourse have *almost* the same structure, which explains our error, induced by Freud himself, in hoping that one day there would be a thermodynamic able to provide – within the future of science – the unconscious with its posthumous explanation.[27]

This reawakens the avant-gardist hope, already played out by the Surrealists, of finding in hysteria not only that prime mover which originally set psychoanalysis into motion, but also a principle of inner contradiction preventing the discourse of psychoanalysis from reaching a premature closure by opting for reductive scientism. By scientism, I mean of course a scientific ideology and not the course of actual science. For instance, Freud's biologism or his dynamism of a libido considered as a sort of steam, a nervous energy produced by the engine of the Unconscious, is obviously a nineteenth-century fantasy, whereas we have learned from Gödel and Heisenberg that scientific models now follow other paradigms dominated by contradiction, incompletion, or uncertainty. Bruce Fink has pointed out how the discourse of the Hysteric paves the way to the discourse of science, and how it is closer to truth than the discourse of the University:

Whereas the university discourse takes its cue from the master-signifier, glossing over it with some sort of trumped-up system, the hysteric goes at the master and demands that he or she shows his or her stuff, prove his or her mettle by producing something serious by way of knowledge. The hysteric's discourse is the exact opposite of the university discourse, all the positions being reversed. The hysteric maintains the primacy of subjective division, the contradiction between conscious and unconscious, and thus the conflictual, or self-contradictory, nature of desire itself.[28]

This corresponds rather well with the view of science we tend to have now: less a series of bold hypotheses about the universe followed by empirical refutations or verifications, as Popper would have it, than a number of parallel investigations all probing at the same time and from different points of view the paradoxes or aporias of current methodologies, ready to shake all preconceived ideas until one reaches new foundations. Or, in John D. Barrow's terms, one has moved from "Theories of Everything" to a scientific practice working through frontiers and repeatedly jumpstarted by fecund encounters with impossibilities.[29]

Lacan's theory of the four discourses should not be taken as limning the psychology of individual scientists, it does not tend to assert, for instance, that Heisenberg was a closet hysteric. The loaded question of science will be treated in a later chapter, since I believe that the main hystericizing effect of Theory has been in relation to its most immediate other discipline, philosophy. This is where we will need to examine a little more closely Lacan's assertion in the same seminar, that Hegel was the "most sublime of all hysterics" (an insight which gave Slavoj Žižek the title of one of his books in French).[30] The remark does not imply, once more, that Hegel was a hysteric himself, but that his philosophy provides the template for the discourse of the Hysteric. It was made in a discussion of the role played by truth in the discourses of the Master and of the Hysteric and moves on to discuss Hegel:

> One cannot say that *The Phenomenology of Spirit* consists in beginning with *Selbstbewusstein* apparently seized at the most immediate level of sensation, implying that all knowledge knows itself from the beginning. What would be the point of all the phenomenology if something else had not been at stake? . . . What I call the hysteria of this discourse comes precisely from the fact that it elides the distinction which would allow one to realize that even if this historical machine, which boils down to the progression of schools and nothing else, was to reach absolute knowledge, this would just imply annulment, failure, disappearance as the term of what motivates the function of knowledge – namely its dialectic relationship with *jouissance*.[31]

In order to make sense of this complex assessment, it will be inevitable to engage systematically and historically with the philosophical implications of readings partly based on terms provided by Kojève's rediscovery of Hegel in the 1930s. I will reopen the debate of these neo-Hegelian thinkers to show how Theory was borne out of the encounter between a favorable intellectual context and this hystericizing discourse that takes its bearing in some version of Hegel or the Other. Thus, before we decide whether we will drive all the tyrants (Hegel, Lacan, and Theory lumped together) from our shores, we need to historicize the role played by the "most sublime of hysterics": how has Hegel's thought generated "hysteria," and how has this led to a "revolution" in Theory?

1

Genealogy One: Hegel's Plague

Lacan's idea that Hegel was responsible for a theoretical hysteri-cization of philosophy is also what underpins Vincent Descombes's discussion of Kojève's impact in the 1930s.[1] I still believe today that a grounding in the patient reading of Hegel (which includes at least the Preface and some key passages of the *Phenomenology of Spirit*) is, if not a prerequisite, at least an essential step on the way to an understanding of Theory. The text is difficult to be sure, but the effort of teasing out its implications and mastering its dialectical idiom affords a good starting point after which one can maneuver freely in other discourses. In a similar vein, Michael Hardt has noticed that everything in French theory – to which one could add German theory – has tended to hinge around a rejection or an acceptation of Hegel's dialectics of negativity and mediation. The Hegel discussion was also crucial in the debate about Critical Theory which opposed Adorno and Benjamin, a debate that still has momentous consequences today (we will return to it later). Hardt has commented on Deleuze's stubborn anti-Hegelianism in a balanced introduction to Deleuze's works entitled "Hegel and the Foundations of Poststructuralism." He shows there that if the first problem of poststructuralism has been to evade Hegel, the second problem has been not to become Hegelian by that very evasion.[2] Precisely because I entirely agree with this view, I would be wary of generalizing Deleuze's choice of a radical positivity, be it located in difference, affirmation, or new assemblages of desire, to a whole

Deleuze Positivity

generation; in that sense, I would still state that the last century has not been Deleuzian (contrary to what Foucault had claimed) but post-Hegelian.

Another point of departure could be Althusser's rewriting of Marx in the name of "theory": for him, Marx had to be the first serious, that is, "scientific" theoretician. The question then becomes: which Marx? The young Hegelian who devotes brilliant pages of witty literary criticism to his former colleagues in *The German Ideology*, or the observer of early capitalism in Britain who posits that an understanding of the economic basis is as necessary for philosophy as for a revolution? Whatever Marx one chooses, it is difficult avoiding the theses systematized by Althusser, whose main claim to fame (beside strangling his wife in a moment of aberration) was his choice of the heading *"collection théorie"* for the famous series he edited at Maspéro in the 1960s. The general argument for the series ran as follows: Theory would bridge the gap between the conceptual elaboration of the philosophical principles contained in Marx's works and new scientific discoveries, contemporary epistemology, and the history of the sciences. It was indeed a time when the (very) red cover of the *Marxist-Leninist Review* was adorned with a running epigraph from Lenin: "Marx's theory is all powerful because it is true."[3] I will return to Althusser's spectacular orbit in due course, noting simply that the word "Theory" in the last century has been indelibly marked by various waves of neo-Hegelianism, most of which took new disguises in successive Gallic impersonations.

Besides, just as it had been important for Mallarmé to think in German through Hegel so as to read in English Poe's poems, thereby durably transform French poetics and poetry, one can sketch a history of French Theory caught emerging from Bergsonism toward existentialism and beyond to structuralism and then post-structuralism; much of its impetus derives from conceptual reversals and borrowings which only make sense if one follows the many avatars of Hegel. Thus Derrida was not being too frivolous or outrageous when he translated Hegel into *Aigle* in *Glas* to echo Jean Genet's puns on his own name (translated as *genêt–je nais*) duplicating, perhaps without being aware of it, Marcel Broodthaers's invention of a whole museum devoted to collecting artifacts evoking or representing eagles: Hegel's plaster bust should be included in the zany zoology of *la section des aigles* which, thanks to the glorious monumentalization of the "king of birds," should provide an ironical postmodern framework to what remains today of "absolute knowledge."

It has often been noted that what passes in America and England as a typically "French" accent given to Theory consisted mainly in retranslations into English of French versions of some German texts – this being especially true of Heidegger, often felt to be almost unreadable in his native German because of the loaded associations with the Nazi period his texts cannot but help carry with them, but who hopefully might be "saved," reinvented, or rediscovered in translation. While Hegel's thought implies technical difficulties in English, there has been a bifurcation in conceptual choices which has radically separated the "continental" Hegel from his British or American versions. I will try to show how Hegel's thought, often allied with Husserlian or Heideggerian components, has kept feeding the theory machine, which should allow us to grasp the intellectual genesis of Theory.

Logic and Existence

Symptomatically in this context, the first translator who introduced Hegel's texts to a French audience was an Italian, Augusto Vera, who had been Hegel's student in Berlin during the last years of the latter's life and translated his works between 1855 and 1878. The most striking feature in these comprehensive translations is the absence of the *Phenomenology of Spirit*. Vera bypassed it, since what motivated him was to show the construction of a scientific system, moving from the *Logic* to the *Philosophy of Nature*, then the *Philosophy of Spirit* and finally the *Philosophy of Religion*. It is a pity that these first translations are forgotten, for they read well and are accompanied by useful annotations, often notes taken directly during Hegel's lectures. They document the influence of Hegel on the French writers who took notice of him, more often poets than philosophers. These writers will constitute in their turn a myth of radical modernity for theoreticians like Barthes or Kristeva, since Mallarmé, Villiers de

23

l'Isle-Adam, Laforgue, and Breton found endless sources of inspiration in these translations. However, the original sin of the French reception of Hegel was the unexplained omission of the phenomenological beginning of the system, an omission that was repaired with a vengeance by later commentators like Kojève in the 1930s.

The impact of Surrealism and all its splinter groups helped rediscover Hegel in the 1930s, above all because he allowed these writers to engage with history, a concern also heightened by the long flirtation of Hegelianism with Marxism. In 1929 Jean Wahl published *The Unhappiness of Consciousness in Hegel's Philosophy*, a book which explained the *Phenomenology of Spirit* through Hegel's early theological writings. Wahl took into account Kierkegaard's critique of Hegelian scholasticism, which led him to stress the role of alienation and desire and present Hegel as a budding existentialist, almost as the same time as Adorno was confronting himself with Kierkegaard. Wahl saw historical progress as a dialectic of loss and separation, in which immediacy was a model for our wish to recapture objects of desire. Longing would mark subjects all passing through stages of alienation and despair before regaining hope. Hope would be founded upon a belief that history continues its open-ended process. This version of Hegel called up more Ernst Bloch's "principle of hope" than Vera's idea of a scientific system.

Then came the Russian-born Alexandre Koyré, who had also seen the importance of Hegel's early writings but did not oppose them to the totalizing System. Koyré reconciled the dialectics of separation, unhappiness, and striving for reunification with the logical aspect of the doctrine and he stressed the originality of Hegel's conception of time, a time dominated by the future. Time contains the seeds of a knowledge that will expand by establishing links between the future and the past; it is only the present that is experienced as contradictory and full of conflicts. Koyré insisted on the anti-theological aspect of Hegel's philosophy, which he defined not as ontology but as anthropology, elements soon to be dramatically played out by Koyré's friend and disciple, Alexandre Kojève.

Coming like Koyré from Russia, Alexandre Kojevnikoff a.k.a. Kojève, suddenly made Hegel indispensable to a whole generation. His seminars at the École Pratique des Hautes Études delivered yearly between 1933 and 1940 gathered people as diverse as

Raymond Queneau, Georges Bataille, Jacques Lacan, Raymond Aron, Maurice Merleau-Ponty, Jean Desanti, and Jean Hyppolite. Kojève's appeal lay in his uncanny ability to transform Hegel's abstract prose into a lively philosophical novel, to give blood to the notion of a "gallery of images" traversed by the Spirit in the famous image of the penultimate page of the *Phenomenology*. As Descombes puts it:

> Alexandre Kojève was a very talented story-teller. In his commentaries, the austere Hegelian *Phenomenology* turns into a kind of serialized philosophical novel, where one dramatic scene follows another; picturesque characters come face to face, reversals of situation keep up the suspense, and the reader, avid to know the end of the story (or history), clamours for more.[4]

Like Koyré, Kojève first dismisses the religious element in the system so as to stress the anthropological problematic: "According to Hegel – to use the Marxist terminology – Religion is only an ideological superstructure."[5] Kojève's point of departure is the dialectic of the Master and Slave. It is a turning point in the analysis of the discovery of reciprocity between consciousnesses and of the need to be acknowledged by another consciousness that should be free to do so. Thanks to this conceptual lever Kojève brings Marx and Heidegger to bear on the Hegelian dialectic. Starting from the biographical insight that the meeting of Hegel and Napoléon in Jena embodied or allegorized absolute knowledge completed by the writing of the book, Kojève returns to the old historical scandal, well noted by Hegel, that Greek cities invented democracy but never abolished slavery. Such a theoretical contradiction gives fuel to the dynamics of human desire. If man is ready to sacrifice his biological self in order to satisfy his desire for recognition in the fight to death that marked the early times of civilization, one could always find some individuals who accepted servitude rather than lose their life. Thus, after speech, desire, and reciprocity, slavery is the fourth dominant concept in Hegel's anthropology – "the possibility of a difference between the *future* Master and the *future* Slave is the fourth and last premise of the *Phenomenology*."[6] History is put

25

in motion with the difference between masters and slaves and it will end only when this difference is abolished. There again, the system is geared toward the future: consciousness is caught up between a "not yet" and an "always already" without which the hystericizing machine could not be wound up.

Kojève's analysis develops a little drama: the master has risked death in what might appear as a more authentic relationship to his *Dasein* which echoes with Heidegger's *Being and Time.* In fact it is the slave who is more authentic because he is determined in his very being by his "fear of death." After his victory, the master can bask in his superiority and leave everything material to his slave; he will be content with enjoying the benefits of another's labors. The slave, who owns nothing, not even his desire, since he toils to satisfy the master's least whims, will discover another authenticity through productive work which slowly transforms nature, whereas the master has to satisfy himself with the more and more empty recognition of his peers. The truth of the master is thus in the slave: only he can reconcile work and knowledge.

> The Master appears only for the sake of engendering the Slave who "overcomes" or "sublates" (*aufhebt*) him as Master, while thereby "overcoming" himself as Slave. And this Slave who has been "overcome" is the one who is satisfied by what he *is* and will understand that he is satisfied in and by Hegel's philosophy, in and by the *Phenomenology*.[7]

An original element brought forward by Kojève's reading has been revived by Francis Fukuyama in the 1990s[8] and is the most counter-intuitive for common sense: it is the thesis of the end of history, glossed by Descombes as our irrepressible wish to know whether we reach the novel's happy ending (or not) as the end, in short as a purely literary closure. Indeed, if one stresses from the start an anthropological reading which will never lose sight of the problem concretely posed by the realization of Absolute Knowledge posed as the last stage of the progression of Spirit through Time, it seems inevitable to conclude that the attainment of Absolute Knowledge would result in the elimination of anthropology qua anthropology – that is, in the "end of man." A long footnote to

Kojève's 1938–9 seminar states almost off-handedly that this is not an apocalyptic vision, quite the contrary:

> The disappearance of Man at the end of History, therefore, is not a cosmic catastrophe: the natural World remains what it had been from all eternity. And therefore, it is not a biological catastrophe either: Man remains alive as animal in *harmony* with Nature or given Being. What disappears is Man properly so-called – that is, Action negating the given, and Error, or in general, the Subject *opposed* to the object.[9]

In this Edenic reverie, wars and revolutions will slowly but surely disappear, along with Philosophy as the discourse that accompanied them, while all the arts, passions, and the elements of superfluity will be needed so as to fill in an empty time, since we will all be happily enjoying an endless "Sunday of Life" (to quote Queneau's witty novel). Snobbism and the "Japanese" model of polite rituals will play an exemplary role in such a scheme, which will not be lost on Foucault's subsequent Nietzschean musings on the "end of man," even if they appear couched in an anti-Hegelian epistemology.

It would be idle to try to prove that Hegel never entertained such a fantasy of universal idleness: the end of history belongs to the Hegelian legends critically dissected by Jon Steward and his collaborators.[10] For, as Kojève writes in 1948, he did not wish to explain what Hegel himself had meant but to think with him, through him and at times against him. He readily acknowledges that he has unduly stressed the role of the master and slave dialectic because he wanted to "strike people's minds" and offer new propaganda. As Lacan and many others who have approached Kojève testify, he had only contempt for those who satisfied themselves with the role of pure intellectuals, and stubbornly refused all academic honors while most of his life was spent as a high civil servant working on international relations between European states and their former colonies, devising and implementing an original system of aid and compensation. Kojève stands out as a fascinating figure in the present context because he saw globalization loom larger as a consequence of a Hegelian system which would be identical with a society dominated by technology and capital; this is why he perceived in potential conflicts between North and South or between the "first" and the "third" worlds more fundamental issues than class conflicts still thought of in terms of industrialization and infrastructure versus superstructure in classical Marxist theory. For him, the Chinese revolution was not a new departure but just the sign that "the provinces were toeing the line" – and, no doubt, he would have said the same of the fall of the Berlin wall – that it fulfilled a scheme already provided by Hegel's all too rational system.

Curiously, the same starting point would lead an eager disciple of Kojève like Bataille in an opposite direction, since he took expenditure and waste as counter-levers in a negative economy of spending – an economy leading to the assertion of death, sacrifice, and excess by which, hopefully, capitalist rationality would meet its undoing or its "othering." The young Bataille was nevertheless completely Kojèvian, as one can see in the mimetic and adulatory tone of his "Letter to X., lecturer on Hegel."[11] His analyses only make sense if one translates "Hegel" as "Kojève's vision of Hegel." Like Kojève, Bataille would be marked by a Romantic Hegel and he never tires of quoting the famous description of man as a "night," "a night that one perceives if one looks a man in the eyes; then one is delving into a night which becomes terrible; it is the night of the world which then presents itself to us."[12] One could say that the whole of Maurice Blanchot's extraordinary novel *Thomas the Obscure* (especially in the first version of 1941) is a gloss on these dense and startling lines. In light of this pervasive Romanticism, it would be useful to compare Bataille's text with an early essay by Althusser, "Man, That Night" (1947), actually a critical review of Kojève's Hegel notes. Althusser is obviously impressed by Kojève's anthropological developments of Hegelian dialectics, even if he is not convinced by Kojève's presentation of an "existentialist Marx" (by which he means a Hegel filtered by Heidegger), a "travesty in which Marxists will not recognize their own."[13] However, the general assessment is generous, which is quite striking in view of Althusser's later position: not Heidegger, but Hegel "is the mother-truth of contemporary thought. Reading Kojève, one might say that this holds for Marx too – that Marx emerges from Hegel fully armed with the dialectic of master and slave."[14] And in a more ominous whisper, Althusser suggests that this dialectic is where Kojève soon meets his limits.

In spite of Kojève's obvious brilliance and seduction, there was a need for a more scholarly examination of Hegel, which was soon provided by Jean Hyppolite. He began by translating into French the whole *Phenomenology of Spirit*, only available in fragments until then, to which he added a systematic running commentary. He then attempted a synthesis between the earlier and the later Hegel in *Logic and Existence*, a collection that brought about a reversal of perspective leading to the increased stress on science and logic associated with the emergence of structuralism in philosophy. Theory as we know it today is inseparable from this momentous philosophical transformation of Hegelianism. Hyppolite's impact may be gauged when one observes how Lacan slowly moved from a Kojevian version of Hegel stressing desire, mirror images, and aggressivity, to a more complex vision in which negativity, language, science, and a pervasive Otherness seem to be generated by direct discussions with Hyppolite who regularly participated in his Seminar in the 1950s. When Lacan states that "Man's desire is desire of the Other," he is in fact glossing Hyppolite's use of "The Other" for the object of desire understood as pure alterity or just "Life." Unlike Kojève, Hyppolite does not see in desire one of the most fundamental concepts in Hegel. And of course, very early in his commentary, he refuses the idea that history might have an end, for him a very naive belief that the system is in a position to freeze history. Hegel famously asserts in the Preface to his *Philosophy of Right* that it is "just as absurd to fancy that a philosophy can transcend its contemporary world as it is to fancy that an individual can overleap his own age," an idea echoed at the end of André Breton's *Nadja*. Accordingly, Hyppolite stresses the experience of joy and pain in the present, and the awareness that the consciousness progressing through various stages in the *Phenomenology* implies both a singular and a universal consciousness.

Hyppolite, who knew the *Phenomenology* by heart as it were, never forgot the systematicity of Hegel's thought. If Hegel's thought forms a system, what is the function of the introduction to knowledge constituted by the *Phenomenology*? Why do we have to follow all the divisions and illusions of a consciousness on its way to absolute knowledge, if absolute knowledge is presupposed from the start? This was Lacan's recurrent worry, as we have seen: can we reach absolute knowledge as a true intellectual goal without sacrificing absolute *jouissance*? On this account, one may say that while the *Phenomenology* is the most literary of Hegel's texts, it is caught up in a tension between "panlogicism" on the one hand and "pantragicism" on the other. Wahl had chosen to stress the tragic, even pathetic elements in the young Hegel, as did Georges Bataille, who sees Hegel as the philosopher of a personal struggle with death and pure negativity. Hegel also looks at real history and its "slaughter-bench" without flinching, as the young Marx had noted with admirative approval. Unlike earlier Hegelians who looked to the German philosopher as a springboard from which they would gain a fresh understanding of History, Hyppolite does not downplay the theoretical risks incurred by a philosophy of history which identifies the Real and the Rational: one may soon fall into a history of the legitimization of political power, and tragic negativity will eventually be sublated or subsumed by the patience of an overarching concept corresponding to the absolutization of the status quo. This explains why Hyppolite sees the core of the *Phenomenology* not in the master and slave dialectic but in Hegel's interpretation of "Terror" during the French Revolution.

A new critical step was reached when Hyppolite published *Logic and Existence* in 1952[15] to tackle the problem of the relationship between the genesis of consciousness in the *Phenomenology* and the structure of the concept contained in the *Logic*. This text is a watershed because it marks a break with the anthropological readings of Hegel that had dominated before World War II, and opts resolutely for an almost Heideggerian version of Hegel. If the Logic presupposes the experience of the phenomenon, and if the phenomenology presupposes the concept, none can be reduced to the other, both are related to the fact that Man is "the dwelling of the Universal and of the Logos of Being, and thus becomes capable of Truth."[16] Hyppolite is at his most Heideggerian here and seems to have read Heidegger's 1930–1 lectures on *Hegel's Phenomenology of Spirit*[17] when he writes: "The Logic's dialectical discourse will be the very discourse of Being, the *Phenomenology* having shown the possibility of bracketing man as natural *Dasein*."[18] The Logic bequeaths us a fundamental insight into the function of sense: Being is thought absolutely, but only through our existence. An essential difference will therefore constitute the very core of Being: Being projects constantly its own Other, unfolds and generates an inner self-differing. Alert as he was to the Nietzschean and Heideggerian echoes of this thesis, Hyppolite paves the way to Derrida's and Deleuze's different philosophies of Difference. However, Hyppolite will not follow to its logical end the implications of Heidegger's displacement, which consists in asserting that in striving for absolute knowledge Hegel never believes that he has reached it, as Kojève tended to think, but forces thinking to think differently by suggesting an experience of rigorous thinking. The shift is mostly grammatical, changing an adjective into a pronoun, which is not "dialectical" in itself: in transforming thinking into a process and an experience, we should not forget to think *absolutely*. This solves the riddle by which Lacan was apparently baffled in the text I have quoted in the last chapter.

Grammatical difference thus sends us to ontological difference, but on a path that forces us to consider the equivalence between being and difference. Deleuze immediately noted this point in a famous review of Hyppolite's work, in which he claimed that, for Hyppolite, "Being is not *essence* but *sense*," which allows him to see how Hegel "transforms metaphysics into logics, and logics into a logics of sense."[19] Which entails that the Absolute is *here*, or in other words, that there is "no secret." This move resembles the strategy that marks Derrida's earlier essays, in which the influence of Husserl is mediated by readings of Heidegger and the impact of Hyppolite's revisionist readings of Hegel. If one examines these essays, one sees how, by taking his bearings in Husserl's attacks on a historicism still identified with Hegelianism, he points out important similarities in Husserl's and Hegel's treatment of language. This is how Derrida sums up Husserl's theses on the ideality of words – I will quote the text and its footnote so as to highlight the complexity of Derrida's strategies, which both assert and undo the thesis of the Husserlian ideality of meaning in the name of a Hegelian theory of language:

Thus, the word has an ideal Objectivity and identity, since it is not identical with any of its empirical, phonetic, or graphic materializations. It is always the *same* word which is meant and recognized through all possible linguistic gestures. Insofar as this ideal object confronts language as such, the latter supposes a spontaneous neutralization of the factual existence of the speaking subject, of words, and of the thing designated. Speech, then, is only the practice of an immediate eidetic.★

★The linguistic neutralization of existence is an original idea only in the technical and thematic signification that phenomenology gives it. Is not this idea the favorite of Mallarmé and Valéry? Hegel above all had amply explored it. In the *Encyclopedia* (one of the few Hegelian works that Husserl seems to have read), the lion already testifies to this neutralization as an exemplary martyr: "Confronting the name – Lion – we no longer have either an intuition of such an animal or even an image, but the name (when we understand it) is its simple and imageless representation; in the name we think" (§462). This passage is cited by Jean Hyppolite in his *Logique et Existence: Essai sur la Logique de Hegel* . . . p. 39, a work which, on many points, lets the profound convergence of Hegelian and Husserlian thought appear. // Hegel also writes: "The first act, by which Adam is made master of the animals, was to impose on them a name, i.e., he annihilated them in their existence (as existents)" (System of 1803–1804). Cited by Maurice Blanchot in *La Part du Feu* . . . p. 325.[20]

In this clever montage of references, Hegel and Husserl converge when affirming the idea that the word is the death of the thing, even if the dramatized idiom of Hegel is foreign to the technicality of Husserl's analysis. Derrida's deconstructive project implies from the outset a patient rereading of Hegel in order to prevent Hegelianism from creeping back into philosophy without warning. He says as much when introducing a critical discussion of Bataille by meditating on a remark by Bataille that Hegel is too "self-evident": "Misconstrued, treated lightly, Hegelianism only extends its historical domination, finally unfolding its immense enveloping resources without obstacle. Hegelian self-evidence seems lighter than ever at the moment when it finally bears down with its full weight."[21] Derrida's assessment of Bataille is harsh: his wish to replace "mastery" by "sovereignty" or to undo servile knowledge in the peals of a laughter capable of shattering metaphysical ghosts seems even more Romantic than Kojève, and downplays both the function of writing and Hegelian negativity.

On the whole, this strategy sketches Derrida's attitude facing Levinas: he plays the devil's advocate, that is the Hegelian figure of a negativity which is so cunning that it has pervaded even the material basis of writing. It's then child's play to demonstrate that one cannot just "leave" the system of philosophical language and "Greek" concepts behind. To leave one's words or work behind, one has to inscribe oneself willy-nilly in a language whose very roots (including basic terms like "Same" and "Other") have been contaminated by dialectical negations and negations of negations. Even the effort to change the whole ground of thinking by presenting us with the face of the other, in a radically new and ethical encounter, has been thought in advance: "The other, for me, is an ego which I know to be in relation to me as an other. Where have these movements been better described than in *The Phenomenology of the Mind?*"[22] There is therefore no possibility of promoting a radical phenomenology of the other's face that would free itself from the encroachments of a Logic whose circle seems all but unbreakable.

Logic and Existence staged an apparent recantation of its author about the respective merits of Hegel's Phenomenology or his Logic, significantly rendering obsolete previous anthropological readings of Hegel, like Kojève's dramatization of the confrontation between Napoléon and the Philosopher of Absolute Knowledge. As we have seen, in 1953 Hyppolite's decision was to return to the loaded relationship between Hegel's logic, a "logic of sense" or pure relations, without leaving behind the stages in the progression of the consciousness sketched by the phenomenology. The new stress on logic and language eventually relegated the ontology of existence or essence to a previous horizon of thought. What mattered then was less ontological difference than the conditions by which sense could be produced, as Deleuze would point out in his groundbreaking review of Hyppolite's new work. Philosophy would not only turn into an ontology of sense, but sense itself would be defined, in Deleuze's words, as "the absolute identity of being and difference."[23] The new generation that included Foucault, Derrida, and Deleuze would take bearings in this intelligent repositioning of Hegel's thought.

We notice that Blanchot was quoted by Derrida in the same passage of his *Introduction* to Husserl's essay on Geometry, although Blanchot seems to belong to a different world, closer to Bataille's or Kojève's readings of Hegel. In his commentary on Husserl's *The Origin of Geometry* Derrida refers decisively to Blanchot's famous essay on "Literature and the Right to Death" which closes *La Part du feu* (1949), a piece providing a theoretical core and largely based upon a reading of Hegel. If Kojève is still felt to be an authority on Hegel (he is quoted as having shown how Marx and Hegel agree fundamentally, and he has demonstrated that "understanding is the equivalent of a murder"),[24] Blanchot also relies heavily on Hyppolite's *Genesis and Structure of the Phenomenology of Spirit* to point out that the main political discovery in Hegel is not the issue of slavery but that of the Terror during the French Revolution: the Marquis de Sade becomes a paradoxical hero who had confronted death and Terror directly.

Fundamentally, Blanchot starts from Hegel to explore some paradoxes that any writer will have to face, and the first is, typically, the impossibility of really beginning (as Hegel had significantly complicated the issue of "beginning" the discovery of knowledge).

> From his first step, as Hegel says more or less, the individual who wants to write is blocked by a contradiction: in order to write, he needs the talent to write. But in themselves, talents are nothing. So long as he has not sat at a table and written a work, the writer is not a writer and he does not know whether he has the ability to become one. He has talent only after he has written, but he needs talent to write.[25]

Caught between two impossibilities the writer becomes, following another Hegelian phrase, a nothingness working with nothingness. This is the kind of Hegelian paradox Blanchot relishes − they are less glib than it seems for they will soon lead to Roland Barthes's concept of an "intransitive" writing understood as pure process, without any consideration of talent or even of creating an *oeuvre*.

Beyond the Hegelian references that structure the logical form of the argument, one sees another reference looming larger in Blanchot's text: it is Levinas, who provides not so much a way out as another terminology to move out from the pathetic mazes of negativity. Levinas introduces an abyssal foundation linking Hegel's "Man as Night" to a "there is" in its matt neutrality. Levinas's thought is obsessed by the wish to exceed the circle of consciousness, by an attempt to leave the entire language of phenomenology behind, a "step beyond" whose difficulty and aporia have been stressed by Derrida. Levinas finds an unexpected ally in Sartre, who criticized Hegel's "ontological optimism" which made him trust Totality too easily. In fact, the Whole had already been given at the outset. Sartre then remarked ominously: "But if Hegel forgets himself, we cannot forget Hegel."[26]

The same obsession with Hegel returns in the later Merleau-Ponty. In his posthumous *Lecture Notes* as well as in the unpublished essay he had called *An Introduction to the Prose of the World*, one can see how Merleau-Ponty's initial debt to Husserl paves the way to a systematic confrontation with Hegel (the very title of "prose of the world" is borrowed from Hegel) and Heidegger. Both thinkers pose the question left unsolved in Husserl of the link between language and historicity, a concern that would also mark Derrida's starting point. It looks as if Husserl and Heidegger had been indispensable mediators helping Merleau-Ponty find how "Hegel and his negativity entered the Flesh of the World."[27] At that time, however, a new French Marxism dominated by Althusser would reject any trace of Hegelianism in the name of the scientific character of Marx's thought. Althusser had remarked, as we have seen, in his 1947 review of Kojève, that the latter's merit had been to show that "without Heidegger . . . we would never have understood the *Phenomenology of Spirit*";[28] the coupling of two of the three H's, Hegel, Husserl, and Heidegger, would soon suffice to brand them as idealist, thus unfit to enter the realm of strict "theory."

After a few false starts (passing through radical Catholicism and Hegelianism) Althusser came into his own as a philosopher by showing how Marx had been able to come into his own as a philosopher. His deduction is almost syllogistic: we know that Marx derives his dialectical method from Hegel and the left Hegelians, that he overturns an idealist way of thinking by putting material determinations first and inverting the inversion. If there is a continuity between the "young Marx" and the mature Marx, Marx himself wants to disentangle scientific theory from ideology. He therefore only reaches scientific rigor when he breaks with the ideological tradition he has inherited from the Hegelians. The "young Marx" is not yet "truly Marx," he is a Fichtean, a Feuerbachian, or worse yet, a humanist. In the name of Bachelard's concept of the "epistemological break," Althusser projects a radical break with the past in Marx, a break that would be situated around 1845. It is hard to understand today why Althusser needed to deploy so much intellectual *savoir-faire* in establishing what looks either like a tautology (Marx is "scientific" when he puts "science" first) or an arbitrary chronological divide (since there might be more than one "jump" or "break" in Marx's discovery of economic rationality). It would be snide to refer this obsession with purity to an undigested Catholicism suggesting a violent and radical conversion, the need to separate the Old dispensation from the New gospel of science and theory, and the rejection of contested texts like *The 1844 Manuscripts* because they would be ideologically suspect. It is more relevant to see how such a theoretical fervor could only spread in a heavily charged political context: after the denunciation of Stalinism by Khrushchev, the official ideology of the Communist Party had tried to become more open by embracing humanism. In France, this seduction operation promoted a weak form of Marxist humanism as less threatening for the new middle class. Althusser's rigorous distinctions were instrumental in providing the rising group of the French Maoists with a new philosophy in which scientism and Stalinism could go hand in hand; meanwhile, Althusser would stay on the margins of the Communist Party.

Baltimore 1966 and After

We are now reaching the fatidic date of 1966 – a turning point or a high tide marked by the publication of theoretical bestsellers: Lacan's *Ecrits* and Foucault's *The Order of Things*, both of which followed hard after the success of Althusser's *For Marx* a year earlier.

In order to knot together all these historical loose braids, I will focus on the conference of the same year which launched French theory in America. One more link with Hegelian sub-plots consists in the fact that the Baltimore meeting of October 1966 in which Barthes, Lacan, Derrida, Goldmann, Vernant, and Todorov were active participants, was partly organized (from the French side) by Jean Hyppolite. The two successive volumes published from these proceedings mark this important debt by dedicating the contents to Jean Hyppolite, "scholar, teacher and friend of scholars."[29] Indeed, the 1970 collection pays a double homage by adding to the translation of Hyppolite's intervention the original French text in an appendix. In his presentation, Hyppolite sketches the problematic of *Logic and Existence*, showing how Hegel's legacy was double: first an analysis of ordinary language starting from a phenomenology of perception, then an investigation of the structure and architecture of languages with the *Logic*.[30] One can see why Hyppolite is the linchpin or the cornerstone of the whole gathering: not only does he mediate between Derrida and Lacan because of personal ties, but he talks to the issues discussed by American presenters like Richard Macksey, who in his opening address quotes at length Wittgenstein and Peirce, and relates to the main concern coming from the structuralist camp, namely the need to found an architecture of discourses on some stable epistemological basis. Finally, he opens philosophical discourse to literary criticism when he compares the *Phenomenology of Spirit* with Dante's *Divine Comedy*, Cervantes's *Don Quixote*, or Balzac's *Human Comedy*.[31]

What was at stake was the possibility of a unifying method that would correspond to a single field of discourse. Peter Caws had the courage to note, in one of the conference's discussions, that he was disappointed to hear so many "metaphysical" presentations instead of the "methodological" clarifications he was expecting,[32] by which he refers to a seemingly endless debate as to whether language created man or man created language. His worry appears as one of the pervasive symptoms of these times – the wish to bracket off foundational speculation and reach for hardcore methods, whether they apply to myth, literature, language, or society. I too can confess to a similar moment, when as a young student in one of the seminars on linguistics that flourished in post-1968 Paris, I helped expel from the group one Heideggerian dissenter who insisted that we had to ponder why "language speaks" before engaging in any other study. What we requested from our tutor was simply a concise breakdown of Saussure's main concepts and an introduction to Benveniste's conception of "enunciation." Even if we guessed that Heidegger's meditation on language was more fundamental than binary categories, what we craved for was *that* technical rhetoric and not the other.

Before engaging in more detail with the 1966 conference itself, it may be useful to remark on the surprising chiasmic reversal one observes between the first and the second title: the decision to use the subtitle as a title not only demotes the philosophical problematic consisting in the articulation between two plurals – "the Languages of Criticism" and the "Sciences of Man" – but promotes a more political or sociological debate, the singular of a "Structuralist Controversy." The new preface written in 1971 spells out what was palpable in 1966, although not clearly perceived by the American public: the lack of a firm agreement between most French theoreticians about the most fundamental issues. But in 1971 it was urgent to recall that structuralism had been questioned or abandoned by some of its alleged practitioners. The 1971 preface quotes Deleuze, who takes Foucault as an example to point out some commonalities of thought that would nevertheless bypass superficial divergences or last-minute mood swings: "A cold and concerted destruction of the subject, a lively distaste for notions of origins, lost origins, recovered origins, a dismantling of unifying pseudo-syntheses of consciousness, a denunciation of all the mystifications of history performed in the name of the progress of consciousness and the unfolding of reason."[33] Foucault had been notoriously absent from the 1966 conference, although quoted here and there, and his genealogical project could still appear as structuralist enough in *The Order of Things*, at least in the concluding remarks presenting the current "human sciences" as obsessed with the notion of structure and structuration – if only with the aim of showing how "man" was less a subject than a vanishing object in these "sciences."

In 1971, however, it was impossible to miss the strictures publicized with *The Archeology of Knowledge* in 1969. Foucault acknowledged that he had unduly stressed discursive synchronicity at the expense of human agency, reducing the "structuralist controversy" to the level of mediatic hype in his unique way:

> So I did not want to carry the structuralist enterprise beyond its legitimate limits. And you must admit that I never once used the word "structure" in *The Order of Things*. But let us leave our polemics about "structuralism"; they hardly survive in areas now deserted by serious workers; this particular controversy, which might have been so fruitful, is now acted out only by mimes and tumblers.[34]

The 1971 preface of the conference proceedings explains the onset of a general dissatisfaction with a model heretofore considered universal, the epistemological paradigm provided by structural linguistics. Two factors not necessarily linked, the "declining methodological importance of linguistics" and "the paradoxical displacement of the role which Hegel had previously occupied,"[35] are adduced by Macksey and Donato to account for the transformation. Hyppolite's untimely death sounded the death knell of Hegelian synthesis, then replaced by a general Nietzscheism quite visible in Foucault, Derrida, and Deleuze.

In fact, even if there is a sort of knee-jerk anti-Hegelianism in Foucault and Deleuze, the deep impact of Derrida's meditation on language and death not only takes up the legacy of a Blanchot but rewrites the Hegelian hesitation between consciousness and logics (as pointed out by Hyppolite) in slightly different terms. It is the extent of this critical difference that I will try to measure here, and the almost ineluctable Hegelian inflection given to any discourse that presents itself as "literary Theory." Moreover, if one examines the proceedings of the 1966 Baltimore conference without any preconceptions, one can see that the most revealing tensions and faultlines do not follow the broad ideological division already mentioned between "methodological" (or structuralist if not scientist) and "metaphysical" (read, if you want, Hegelian) discourses. In fact, the science which is brought to the fore from the start is mathematics, much more than linguistics or generalized semiology seen as global theory of signs. This was due to the impact of the historian Charles

Morazé's presentation, which focused on the "differences between mathematical and literary invention."[36] In a brilliant anticipation of the Sokal debate of the 1990s, Lacan was quick to take his cue: Morazé's introduction of "the root of minus one"[37] described as a completely irrational symbol nevertheless provided an adequate solution to specific problems. Returning to the need for arbitrary symbols invented in moments of crisis or of passionate decision, Lacan poses the question of the distinction between the subject and the living individual: "What is the order of passions around which this event will or will not occur, whatever it may be, this algorithm, invention of a new sign or of a new algorithm or a different organization of some logical systems?"[38] It is evident that what Lacan and most theoreticians invited to the conference insist upon is less the universality of semiotics understood as the science of all signs, than the logical construction of signifying systems in which we are caught and from which the exact function of the subject can be calculated.

The calculable or incalculable nature of the subject remains therefore the crucial divide in these discussions. At one point, Lacan quotes Derrida's query to him: "Why do you call *this* the subject, this unconscious? What does the subject have to do with it?"[39] In a quirky and freewheeling improvisation, Lacan proceeds to narrate an anecdote to illustrate his view of subjective agency. He needed his table moved to another part of his hotel room and had to ask the bellman to do it; to which the bellman indignantly replied that this was a job for the housekeeper. When housekeepers came and performed the task, they did this absent-mindedly, paying no heed to Lacan, only mindful of their hierarchical superiors. This showed to him that he would have been deluded to believe that in this set of actions, he was involved as a subject who makes a request and is obeyed. The experience showed on the contrary that a number of communication misfires and infelicities were necessary. It forced Lacan to immerse himself into the hotel's specific regulations, hierarchies, and power grid; in short an entire Kafkaian universe, including the Law, institutions, even the big Other. Facing such a structure, Lacan could dispel the illusion of the subject's direct agency and show how the subject was a function of the lack implied by a disorder no sooner created than negated. What remained of subjectivity would just be his superfluous impatience in the whole affair.[40]

Lacan's presentation itself did not go down very well: he made the mistake of speaking partly in wrongly accented English and partly in opaque French, the result being that he was poorly understood. Even without these obstacles, the text itself parades its impenetrability from the very labyrinthine title: "Of Structure as an Inmixing of Otherness Prerequisite to Any Subject Whatever." As Lacan confided, he had worked for fifteen years on these problems and could not hope to convey his findings all at once.[41] He nevertheless provided a few forceful images, all allegorizing his immediate surroundings. For instance, describing the view from his hotel at dawn, with blinking neon signs and heavy traffic, he presented this as a reminder that we live in a man-made chaos controlled by signs in which subjectivity often finds itself at a loss: "The best image to sum up the unconscious is Baltimore in the early morning."[42] Besides numerous allusions to Frege and Russell's logical theories, central tenets of Lacan's doctrine are reiterated and glossed: he explains that his old idea that the unconscious is "structured as a language" is a tautology because "structured" and "as a language" are synonymous.[43] More cryptic is the idea that a sign represents something for somebody while a signifier represents a subject for another signifier.[44] Taking another cue from billboard signs displaying "Enjoy Coca-Cola," Lacan points to the irreducible function of *jouissance* beneath desire. Like the soft-drinks industry, our superego forces us to enjoy always more. But if language structures human desire by representing what is forbidden, one should not forget that without the particular excess of a *jouissance* bordering on pain, life would not be worth living.

[handwritten margin note: Sfer-ego]

When we later hear Rosolato expand Lacan's concepts, it is striking to see him mention the linguistic theory not of Saussure but of Benveniste, who allows him to move from Jakobsonian "shifters" to an opposition between "the subject of the enunciation" and the "subject of the enounced." Like Rosolato and Tzvetan Todorov, who moved skillfully from Bakhtin to Benveniste and the Russian Formalists, Roland Barthes also quotes Benveniste rather liberally. All three agree that a crucial task for linguistics is to describe the formal apparatus of enunciation, that is the set of coded devices allowing

41

a person to say "I" or write "I." We should not forget that these terms had been introduced systematically in Lacan's *Four Fundamental Concepts of Psycho-Analysis*, a seminar he gave in 1964. There is a general agreement between Lacan, Rosolato, and Barthes to restrict subjectivity to the simple function of being able to say "I." The linguistic theory to which they all refer hinges on the question of *enunciation*, that is the systemic determinations by which persons, tenses, and voices are expressed in language. The speaking subject will be made and unmade in this linguistic hole through which he or she emerges at the time of a statement before fading away. This development was largely ignored by most Anglo-Saxon commentators, who still tend today to rehash Saussure's basic definitions and binary oppositions (often limited to three: synchrony/diachrony, *langue/parole*, and signifier/signified) as if these alone provided a universal key for the understanding of Lacan, Derrida, and Barthes in the late 1960s. The image of structuralism presented in 1966 to the American public was clearly more complex, sophisticated, and diverse in its epistemologies and strategies than what has often been said.

The really dissenting voices were limited to two: Paul de Man and Jacques Derrida. In retrospect, Paul de Man appears as the most brutal interlocutor facing the French group. He aims his barbs at Barthes, for instance, in quite a scathing way. Embarrassingly, he is almost always right. He tells Barthes rudely: "I must admit, I have been somewhat disappointed by the specific analyses that you give us. I don't believe they show any progress over those of the Formalists, Russian or American, who used empirical methods, though neither the vocabulary nor the conceptual frame that you use."[45] The first accusation is wounding – and touches upon an important fact: much of the French enthusiasm for literary theory had to do with the unleashed energy of recently converted critics who ignored a much longer tradition of critical analysis like that of the Russians or the Americans. The more serious accusation bears on willful distortion of literary history. De Man continues: "when I hear you refer to facts of literary history, you say things that are false within a typically French myth. I find in your work a false conception of classicism and romanticism . . . you distort history *because* you need a historical myth of progress to justify a method which is not yet

42

able to justify itself by its results."[46] Barthes is forced to a lame retreat, and he admits that for him literary history is another kind of myth. De Man has no difficulty in pointing out that the Romantics and even some classics had already expressed what Barthes identifies with a "modern" sensibility limited to an axis of Mallarmé–Sollers.

De Man similarly reproaches Hyppolite for having omitted Hegel's meditation on death and negativity: "You didn't speak of the moment of negation, nor of what seems to me to remain central in Hegel, namely the problem of death."[47] In a wonderful extemporized disquisition on death and radical finitude, Hyppolite answers by stating his fundamental disagreement with Hegel on the central issue of the equivalence between death and negativity. For Hegel, death is too glibly transformed into negation, which is how he can fuel the dialectical engine. If we discover on the contrary that negativity is death, death cannot be redeemed as just a "lost meaning" – like the lost passion deployed by the *schöne Seele* who shatters its sanity by fighting against the world, and whose effort is indeed recuperated or thought through by the philosopher. For Hyppolite, in an admission that life resists the process of intellectual sublation, one should acknowledge that "in any case there is something which is not redeemable, and I would not follow Hegel to the end; I can't."[48] A remarkable affirmation coming as it did from one of the best commentators on Hegel, this brought his discussion to a closure.

Symptomatically, Paul de Man inscribed his question in the context of what he took to be Hyppolite's response to Derrida, whereas Hyppolite was answering Georges Poulet. This apparent slip of the tongue[49] reveals a growing affinity; it was a similar issue that had been brought up earlier by Derrida after Roland Barthes's presentation. Returning to an issue brought by Barthes – of the "impossible" utterance of "I am dead" – Derrida refers to Poe's Mr. Valdemar story and uses this argument to question the linguistic foundation of the semiotics displayed in Baltimore. As we have seen, the basis was less Saussure than Benveniste's theories of *discours* and *récit*: the first would be marked by subjective enunciation, while historical narrative tends to suppress subjective markers. Following his own investigations of Husserl and also going back to Saussure,

Derrida refuses the distinction, since for him there is no more a "pure present" than "pure presence": historical time is always implied in the time of enunciation.[50] Some form of writing, there- fore of death, is always at play in any first-person discourse. When I repeat "I" – which is necessary for the constitution of subjectiv- ity – I have been "absented" from my speech, there is no experi- ence of the radically singularly new and personally authentic that would not be attacked by such a primary repetition. "If the repe- tition is original, that means that I am not dealing with the radi- cally new in language. You were reticent about saying 'I am dead.' I believe that the condition for a true act of language is my being able to say 'I am dead.'"[51] This "death" which may be dramatic or quite bland will be a precondition in order to use language. Derrida follows Hyppolite, who had questioned Barthes's idea of a "pact of speech" when applied to writing.[52] For Derrida, the belief in a pure speech is a fantasy, a delusion under which Barthes is still working. What finally links Derrida and Hyppolite is a Hegelianized Freudi- anism in which death remains unredeemable but nevertheless trig- gers the work of mourning so central in the constitution of the work of art.

Why is it then that Derrida and de Man emerge as the most trenchant participants in the theoretical debate? They both seem more faithful to an earlier and more radical Hegelianism, and both start from an experience of discourse marked by death and nega- tivity. They also insist on the linguistic materiality which could be glossed away in the name of a logic of sense. They refuse to forget the rhetorical, linguistic, or material status of this experience as con- ditioned by language. Can one say that they return to Kojève's Hegel, a thinker for whom death is the absolute Master? Not exactly, since here death underwrites a linguistic process underpin- ning the whole of literature, culture, and the constitution of sub- jectivity. Theory is thus both aware of the idealizing mechanisms propagating "fantasies" and of the quest for the most hidden mate- riality, a materiality in which death finally lurks.

The debate has returned in the vehement discussion which has opposed Lacan's theses on the "letter" in his seminar on Poe's "Pur- loined Letter" and philosophical critiques coming from Derrida,

Althusser, Lacoue-Labarthe, or Nancy.[53] When Derrida and Althusser find themselves in agreement facing what they denounce as Lacan's idealizing gesture, they share an identical suspicion facing the consensus that seems to emerge from the Baltimore proceedings. Nevertheless, despite irreducible divergences, both Lacan and Barthes on the one hand, Derrida and de Man on the other, with Hyppolite somewhere in the middle, testify to the overwhelming power of a Hegelianized Theory at that time. We have seen that it is impossible to define Theory without taking into account its effects in a given historical context. This was also Althusser's position facing a Lacan he did not really "like" but admired for his theoretical effort. In a very illuminating letter to the psychoanalyst René Diatkine, Althusser put forward Lacan's historical role:

> Lacan's claim and his unique originality in the world of psychoanalysis lie in his being a *theoretician*. Being a theoretician does not mean producing a theoretical concept corresponding to an empirical, clinical, practical fact, or even *several* theoretical concepts; it means producing a *general system* of the theoretical concepts, rigorously articulated with each other and capable of accounting for the *total set* of facts and of the field of analytic practice.[54]

Althusser knew from Diatkine and other psychoanalysts that the "character" of Lacan might not be up to scratch or might even provoke violent personal resistances – but, still in the name of sacrosanct Theory, he was ready to make crucial allowances; when Diatkine expressed reservations with Lacan the man, Althusser swept them away:

> You will answer me with the individual Lacan, but that is not what is at stake: it is a matter of his work, and even beyond his work, it is a matter of that which it is the sole extant proof: it is a matter of the *existence* in principle of theory in the field of psychoanalysis. Paris was well worth a mass. . . . the individual Lacan, his "style" and his idiosyncrasies and all the effects they have produced, including the personal wounds –

all that "*is well worth theory.*" There are some goods for which one never pays too much, the very ones that bring more than they cost.[55]

Was Paris then really worth the structuralist mass? In fact the high cost or the subtle danger were indeed not bounded by people's personal flaws or even by the cult of personality lurking in Lacan or others – the real risk was that, as the song says, Paris would remain only Paris.

2

Genealogy Two: The Avant-Garde at Theory's High Tide

I have so far stressed the impact of Hegel in my genealogy of what has come to be called Theory in the United States and Britain, and now need to confess that I may have overstressed the links, derivations, and cross-references to what is, after all, a pervasive but rather vague philosophical tradition. Hegelianism, a scare-word for Russell and Wittgenstein, is not identical with Hegel's works, those challenging texts into which one has to dip and plunge often. Besides, since my aim is less to offer a survey of the past than a number of suggestions for the future, I would like to insist on how three main theoreticians – who not only loom large in last century's context but also set down the lineaments of Theory for this one – have variously resisted Hegelian categories.

Perhaps driven by an anaphoric undertow similar to a movement that pushed me further and further in quest of the canonical three H's of German philosophy, I will restrict my investigation to the no less canonical figures who can be called the three B's of Theory: Benjamin, Bakhtin, and Barthes. Although it would be a stretch to claim that they make up the canon of Theory, I have found in my teaching experience that a thorough familiarity with their works and careers provides the most important concepts, texts, and issues. I do believe that their impact will continue to be felt well into this century. Beyond anaphoric onomastics (however shared with Bataille, Blanchot, and Bhabha) they do have one major common feature: their works are so abundant, diverse, and contradictory that one of the pleasures yielded by their challenging and exciting texts is that one cannot fail to discover incompatible doctrines in them. Barthes has been variously catalogued as a structuralist scientist and as a non-committed hedonist in the great French lyrical and auto-biographical tradition, a neo-Marxist doubled by a queer theoretician in disguise who ended up a poststructuralist, a novelist *manqué* with a wistful fascination for the avant-garde, a deep nostalgia for Romanticism, and a real Proustian complex. Benjamin, a Marxist critic who never read Marx, appears at times closer to linguistic mysticism or Jewish messianism, while his neo-Kantian beginnings jar with his later endorsements of Brecht or the Russian revolution. His impact on the emergence of a new modernist canon has been unequaled, though, while his whole work alone justifies the preponderance of a vibrant neo-Marxist school of criticism in the twenty-first century. As for Bakhtin, the issue is even more complex, since the authorship of a number of texts is still disputed, and while the issue is not settled, important essays were written in collaboration, which has generated entire schools of disciples fighting over the archive and the significance one can attribute to Bakhtin's evolution, going from a neo-Kantism to a more open neo-Marxism, from bitter attacks on Saussure and Formalism to a religious humanism that had to use Aesopian language to resist Stalinism, finally culminating in historical vistas that could be seen to announce "cultural studies." Bakhtin has nevertheless remained profoundly marked by the philosophical readings of his youth, from Hermann Cohn's ethics to Buber's dialogics, before finding a subtle way of reconciling the kenotic tradition of Russian Orthodoxy with an idealized pagan hybridity of the Middle Ages praised and monumentalized under various names such as "carnival" or "Menippean satire."

All three writers offer the interesting spectacle of what the French call *une auberge espagnole*, an inn to which you bring what you have to consume. But, by a twist that is characteristic of contemporary Theory, the big open inn has spawned hundreds of small restaurants, each displaying fiercely distinctive menu styles, a distinctiveness undercut by identical B.Y.O.B. signs. If we leave behind all traces of nostalgia for the big inn and opt for the customary round of visits, we just need to remember which bottle to bring in each case; with Barthes no doubt, one would carry along a popular

French red like Côte du Rhone or better Cahors, a heavy wine endowed with a mystical kinship with blood as demonstrated in *Mythologies*, while in order to accompany Benjamin one would probably choose a racier mixture, Spanish *sangre de toro* laced with hashish and tobacco, a tobacco shared by Bakhtin who once notoriously smoked the carbon copies of precious manuscripts, but we would want to add to his favorite black tea some Absolut vodka. Theory often tastes like the haphazard cocktail resulting from the heady mix: it can produce headaches and hangovers, but as Althusser has reminded us, there are some goods for which one never pays too much.

There is, however, a deeper root of affinities which can be linked with a commonly uneasy resistance to Hegelianism. For Benjamin, this came to a head in the crucial debate which opposed him to his friend Adorno in the 1930s, a debate from which not only a clearer definition of Theory emerges, but which shows why, historically speaking, the Frankfurt school and its idea of "critical theory" failed to embody High Theory in spite (or perhaps because) of early success in its American reception. With Bakhtin, it was his lifelong resistance to dogmatic and institutional Marxism that led him to a choice of tactical weapons found first in linguistics, then in literary history and comparative anthropology. While his later work provided the adequate counterpart to British Marxism that went into the formation of "cultural studies," and his earlier essays were so influential for French theory in the 1970s, he stands out as a writer who bypassed dominant Hegelian legacies geared to totalizing dialectics and who invented a new style of interaction between authority and dialogue, thus paving the way to the thinking of a post-communist era marked by the forceful return of ethics rather than religion. Barthes's status as a fellow-traveler of the French Communist Party, who then turned into a guru of the Paris intelligentsia nevertheless not above declaring that "all language was fascistic" at the end of his life, makes the assessment more delicate. If one focuses on his early works, as I will now, one can measure how much of his line of thought is determined by a wish to avoid being trapped by Sartrian dialectics like those I have sketched in chapter 1. I will rapidly examine these three motives in turn before comparing the careers of these thinkers, all of whom moreover remained marginal facing the educational systems and elite institutions. This will lead me to focus on the history of the precarious flirtation of Theory with the avant-garde by evoking the rise and fall of a review that has emblematized for a while the very concept of High Theory: *Tel Quel*. This historical overview should point to what can be "redeemed" (to use a favorite expression of Walter Benjamin's) and what ought to be rejected in the cult of Theory for Theory's sake.

Critical Theory and the Critique of Critique

When one talks about Theory in connection with the idea of a Critique, it looks as if pride of place ought to be given to Adorno's and Horkheimer's Frankfurt school and its well-known insistence on a specific "critical theory," with its very influential legacy to the British and American New Left in the 1960s. Herbert Marcuse at least is one the founders of Theory who should please Camille Paglia, since his very name immediately calls up images of students' demonstrations, anti-Vietnam protests, sit-ins and love-ins, endless discussions about staunch resistance to power and oppression via drugs, sex, and activism, and creative alternatives to the repressive adjustments imposed by a "System" equated with bourgeois society and its repressive apparatus. Then, politics would be a huge caldron into which the names of Reich and Marx, Trotsky and Rosa Luxemburg, Freud and Fromm, and why not Chairman Mao and Norman O. Brown, would be tossed in. This crucial historical priority should be acknowledged. Yet, I subscribe entirely to Sylvère Lotringer's acute analysis when he makes the point that it had been in the name of "critical theory" that "French theory" had been resisted in America, that it had been accused of being either "irrationalist" or "apolitical," when not both. Indeed, after Adorno and Horkheimer had to relocate their Institute for Social Research to Paris in 1933 and then to New York two years later, its discourse was eagerly welcome by avant-garde intellectuals in both capitals. However, its fate came to be markedly different in New York. Here is how Lotringer explains this evolution:

50

The Frankfurt school had permeated the entire American Left. Breaking away from the old Left compromised far too much with the Soviet Union, American-style Marxists had pruned Marxism of some of its major tenets, especially the primacy of class, and now emphasized reification and commodity independently of their conditions of production. Celebrating negativity and disenchantment may have been less a result of Adorno's own negative dialectics than a way of making thinking legitimate in a country otherwise brimming with shoddy optimism. In short, starting from the Frankfurt school, a toothless kind of Marxism had emerged, custom-made for the American academy, of which art critics and art historians were increasingly a part.[1]

One main irony is that the historical bridge established as early as the end of the 1930s between Adorno's modernist theory of negativity in the arts (with a stress on high music and a distaste for low culture) and Clement Greenberg's conception of modernism in painting as a "pure" and "critical" mode of expression became so successful that it would soon provide the New York avant-garde with a coherent discourse serving not only to launch abstract expressionism as the "new" movement but also to "steal" from Paris the function of capital of the living arts, all this to be finally exported back to Europe after World War II. Here were the real counter-models of American cultural supremacy, and they would play the role of a subtle ideological Trojan horse on the other side of the iron curtain. In a time of Cold War politics, jazz, especially a more radically "free jazz" (even though Adorno resented "jazz" – actually Berlin's twenties version of Dixieland – even more than he bore a grudge against Stravinsky for having betrayed modernist aesthetics born intact from Schönberg's thigh) was objectively allied with Pollock's abstract painting in a global showcasing of official American art, so as to herald the triumph of a new way of feeling and living based on American values. In a final effort to throw a sop to Camille Paglia, I quite agree that rock 'n' roll did as much as American capitalism and the Marshall Plan to pull down the Berlin wall. And of course Khrushchev would never have happened without Elvis Presley nor Althusser without the Beatles!

51

One might object to this development that, if all this is true and established, it should not diminish in the least the importance of the Frankfurt school, whose texts one should attempt to reread today with as much care and passion as Hegel's. Rather than serving a series of clichés that tend to present the 1960s as a moment of fun, intoxication, and fuzzy thinking, it would be more worthwhile to reopen the texts of Adorno and Horkheimer. To be sure, if one goes to the selected essays written by Max Horkheimer for the *Zeitschrift für Sozialforschung* in the late 1930s, during and after his Frankfurt years,[2] one can see how they militantly aim at defining and promoting a general "critical theory" in which Marxism and Freudianism are harmoniously compounded. Its main thrust is directed against positivism considered as a bourgeois distortion of a science whose current crisis has not been acknowledged because it has turned into a religion.

Thus the essay on "Traditional and Critical Theory" begins with a parallel between the definition of "theory" in science, which is subject to tests and verification and therefore considered more as a set of hypotheses than dogma, and the use of the term for the sciences of man and society. For the scientific side, Poincaré and Husserl are adduced (Husserl defines theory as "a systematically linked set of propositions, taking the form of a systematically unified deduction")[3] whereas sociology as defined by Durkheim and Weber, as well as the *Geisteswissenschaften* of a Dilthey, force one to acknowledge the links between Kant's "Critiques" of knowledge and critical thought understood as polemical, corrective, and oppositional. This is a knowledge that cannot be divorced from its originator as in stricter and abstract science, since it mobilizes the subjective relationships involving the scientist as a social being. The role of the intellectual facing the proletariat is thus implied: the intellectual should not just perform social psychology or a mimetic sociology, but should aim at a general transformation of society. It is because class differences create some form of mystification that critical theory is needed: "The theoretician whose business it is to hasten developments which will lead to a society without injustice can find himself in opposition to views prevailing even among the proletariat . . . If such a conflict were not possible, there would be no need of a theory."[4] Horkheimer's theory is indeed Marxist in

52

the sense that it acknowledges the priority of class struggle, but it tends to lay the stress on issues of distribution rather than production:

> Thus the critical theory begins with the idea of the simple exchange of commodities and defines the idea with the help of relatively universal concepts . . . Without denying its own principles as established by the special discipline of political economy, the theory shows how an exchange economy, given the condition of men . . . must necessarily lead to a heightening of those social tensions which in the present historical era lead in turn to wars and revolutions.[5]

All this confirms Lotringer's diagnosis, and paves the way for its American recuperation: the politics of class and power will soon be replaced by a sociology of consumption, in which the key concepts of reification, fetishization, alienation, and commodification and the like will keep enough of their Marxist edge without being too compromising.

Not only falling prey to a sociologist bias, the critical theory thus produced is much more Hegelian than Marxist. The theory attempts to understand the realities of liberal capitalism from the model of a commodity economy and will do so by way of a Hegelianized Marx:

> The conceptual development is, if not parallel, at least in verifiable relation to the historical development. But the essential relatedness of theory to time does not reside in the correspondence between individual parts of the conceptual construction and successive periods of history: that is a view on which Hegel's *Phenomenology of the Mind* and *Logic* and Marx's *Capital*, examples of the same method, are in agreement.[6]

In view of the previous discussion of Althusser's epistemological jumps and cuts, one can understand why an apparent dogmatism aimed at dispersing such confusions. One can sympathize with Horkheimer's wish to avoid the trap of economism and postulate a higher totality of thought and action, in which materialist

53

dialectics and historicism can be reconciled. The weakness of this "theory" appeared quite clearly in the collection of essays Horkheimer edited in 1936 on the theme of "Authority and the Family"; accordingly, the longest and most ambitious piece in his *Critical Theory* was included in it. In "Authority and the Family" we have all the seeds of later developments on education and repression in the framework of the bourgeois family. The section on "Authority" is quite typical: after a survey of the various philosophical attempts at destroying the power of authority and authorities in which Descartes, Kant, Fichte, and Nietzsche play a prominent role, it leads directly to a development on the Family because this is the only materialistic basis for such a rejection. Authority is concentrated in the father who ends up embodying the reification of the essence of bourgeois capitalism.

Finally, more than a Marxist thesis (or rather Engelsian analysis, in this context) allied to a Freudian critique with a more committed edge (as one finds in Wilhelm Reich), we are treated to an updated version of Hegel's reading of *Antigone*.[7] However, Horkheimer does not seem to realize that this very example completely contradicts his earlier sociological thesis, since Hegel has shown (and this only for the moment of the Greek city) that if there is a mortal antagonism between the laws of the family and the laws of the state, it is traversed by the logical sexual difference: the laws of the family are in the hands of the women, while the laws of the *polis* are given to the brothers or to the father. A weak Freudo–Marxism finally wraps up the vague Hegelianism: "The authority structure of a particular family, however, can be strong enough for the father to maintain his position even after its material basis has disappeared . . . Psychic and physical power, which grew out of economic power, thus shows its capacity for resistance."[8] It is not astonishing then to see Horkheimer conclude with a quotation from Hegel's *Logic* stressing the dialectical totality of individuality and universality: everything and its contrary have become reunified in a soft synthesis.

It is revealing to compare this text with Lacan's early essay on the Family, a text almost contemporary since it was written in 1936 and published in 1938 in a French encyclopedia. Lacan's entry, about the same length as Horkheimer's, on the "Family complexes in the formation of the individual," was first thought to be so obscure that it had to be rewritten some ten times. In it one will find Lacan's closest approximation to the theses then developed by Bataille's Collège de Sociologie, a group which counted Walter Benjamin as a friendly if ironical and detached member. Lacan's starting point is a description of what he calls "the institution of the family" in order to show that the family has nothing natural or biological and has to be thought of as a fully human "institution."[9] The equivalence between the biological family and the symbolic family is a simple coincidence. This very dense essay where one can find all the seeds of Lacan's future theoretical articulations begins by replacing once and for all the Freudian concept of "instincts" with a dialectic of "complexes": not biological throughout, complexes are buttressed on biological factors, and if they create neuroses they also structure the human psyche. The first "complex" this broad survey focuses on is the weaning process, which always leaves a crucial trace in subjects because of the constitutional immaturity of humans; we have all been weaned before we were self-sufficient. Thus, by the concomitant invention of the Oedipus complex, the family manages to bridge the constitutional gap in the individual with a symbolic hierarchy in which one could find the lineaments of Horkheimer's analysis of authority.

For Lacan, reality itself is constituted after sexuality has been processed and mediated by the family complexes, a process in which death and castration intervene next to jealousy, mimetic rivalry, identification to a specular image, and imaginary captures. Lacan appears very close to Melanie Klein in a compendium of psychoanalytic doctrine allied with references to von Uexküll's theories of animal behavior and Marcel Mauss's analysis of exchange of gifts and women in society. Refining on what might be read as an accusation of the Freudian Father, Lacan notes in passing that authority is often embodied by the maternal uncle in matriarchal societies.[10] To these customs he opposes the Jewish invention of monotheism and its derived sense of paternal authority which links Bergson and Freud, both marked by the paternal imago. Lacan does not denounce like Horkheimer the residue of capitalism lurking in the father's authority, and contents himself with mentioning that anarchists like Proudhon had been deeply marked by the authority they rebelled against.[11] But, in a strange tirade against fathers, Lacan betrays some of his own complexes when he concludes the first part in this way: "Our experience forces us to designate the principal determination [of contemporary neuroses] in the father's personality, which is always somehow lacking, absent, humiliated, divided or fake."[12] When describing the "decline of the paternal imago" Lacan's text is unexpectedly much more violent than Horkheimer's essay: whereas "critical theory" appears as a meek and somewhat lazy Hegelianization of German sociology in the name of Marxism, just peppered by a few zesty but scattered quotes from Nietzsche and Kierkegaard, Lacan's non-critical or more truly "affirmative" synthesis of psychiatry, psychoanalysis, animal ethology, and human sociology evinces a radical subversive force. Here is a dialectical vortex which should convince readers that the theoretical moment is synthetic, totalizing, and above all indispensable. In fact, as Roudinesco explains, Lacan was branded as a Hegelian and Marxist by his masters in psychiatry after the publication of this article: Pinchon was even to assert that Lacan had forgotten not just French grammar but also the semantic distinction between "culture" and "civilization"![13]

A similar misunderstanding took place around the issue of theoretical methods between Adorno and Benjamin, and it illustrates the reasons for critical theory's loss of relevance or diminished impact on the current scene of Theory. Of course, I cannot pretend to make sense of Benjamin's critical strategies in a few pages, and I will just focus on one particular exchange in which the right definition of Theory acquires a crucial weight. In order to prepare for this exchange, it is useful to go back to a slightly earlier essay by Benjamin in which he sketched the contours of German Romantic criticism, with its inflationary use of "critique" in at least two senses: the negative sense of either pointing to the limits of knowledge as with Kant, or of attacking deficiencies in taste or artistic production; the positive one being the wish to make this activity reflexive in a redoubling mirror-image of creation: without criticism understood positively, creation could not know itself as an agency linked to a general process disposing of specific laws.

Noticing how Romantics like the brothers Schlegel and Novalis had given an active and positive sense to the word of "critique," a word which for the Romantics had acquired "an almost magical meaning," Benjamin goes back to the obvious root of this use, Kant's critical mode of operation: "One can therefore say that the concept of criticism has a double sense in Kant – that double sense which in the Romantics is raised to a higher power, since by the word "criticism" they refer to Kant's total historical achievement and not only to his concept of *Kritik*."[14] Criticism comprises the knowledge of its object, but also the knowledge that this knowledge will not suffice, and that this insufficiency is inevitable. A sense of infinity has to come into play, which is of course not the direction Adorno's "critical theory" would take. However, this Romantic infinity will be skewed rather than verticalized in the drift of Benjamin's meditations on literature, culture, and society. In a revealing passage from a letter to Adorno about the latter's book on Wagner, Benjamin opposes Adorno's own mode of approach to music, which he calls "critical," to his own, which he calls "redemptive." He seems painfully conscious that the disclosure of this divergence will perhaps bring a rift between the two friends:

> You must allow me to surprise you in body and soul with your own favourite image from Indian Joe about unearthing a hatchet and provoking a fight – it seems to me that any such salvation, undertaken from the perspective of the philosophy of history, is incompatible with one undertaken from a critical perspective that is focused upon progress and regress.[15]

Benjamin has not only unearthed the war hatchet but begun slicing the rope that had so far connected the two critics. He is right to note that the polemical tone in Adorno's writings is usually based upon a historical concept of progress: for Adorno, Wagner and Stravinsky are "regressive," whereas Schönberg or Beethoven are "progressive" because there is something like a history of forms possessing a logic of its own; if one fails the test of artistic progress, one has to be denounced pitilessly. Benjamin's vision on the other hand, as he sees it, is redemptive or geared toward salvation, even when the material itself is not so "progressive" – whether we talk about the "old form" in Baudelaire's allegories or of the partly meaningless "trash" contained in ancient archives and all sorts of secondary sources. To this process of recuperation or salvation, founded, as we know, on his messianic ideas about the "angel of history," Benjamin gives a cyclical rhythm: "Salvation is a cyclical form, polemic a progressive one."[16]

This bold idea is restated variously throughout the following years, and one incisive formulation appears in the *Arcades Project*: "It may be considered one of the methodological objectives of this work to demonstrate a historical materialism which has annihilated within itself the idea of progress. Just here, historical materialism has every reason to distinguish itself sharply from bourgeois habits of thought. Its founding concept is not progress but actualization."[17] Benjamin's concept of actualization entails the dream of a material culture through which history and texts should illuminate each other reciprocally. However, as he writes in the same *Konvolut N*, while philology underpins the interpretation of texts, theology will have to become the scientific basis of such a method – a provocative statement to be sure. Halfway between material history and theology, this exhaustive reading of a whole period does not denounce reification or fetishization, but on the contrary establishes a whole phantasmagoria of things: reification is not the negative dialectical moment in a view of the progress of history but an imaginative recreation of the given, in a reversal hoping to achieve a redeeming transformation.

With this global theological concern Adorno had very little patience, and felt particularly threatened by the spreading network of myopically close readings of things as texts and of texts as things. If we follow the correspondence about the ill-fated work in progress, the retaliation came swiftly: in a letter mailed from New York in November 1938, Adorno replied with a contained vehemence and bitter sharpness increased by his familiarity with Benjamin's writings – explaining why he could not publish the section of the book on Parisian *passages* (whereas he has asked for a rapid mailing of finished chapters): "Let me express myself in as simple and Hegelian a manner as possible. Unless I am very much mistaken, your dialectic is lacking in one thing: mediation. You show a prevailing tendency to relate the pragmatic contents of Baudelaire's work directly and immediately to adjacent features in the social history, and wherever possible, the economic features, of

the times."[18] What Adorno reproaches Benjamin for is his irrepressible tendency to juxtapose texts and things in the hope of letting
new relationships appear, like Baudelaire's wine poems and contemporary documents about Parisian wine policies or taxation
practices. What is superbly observed and dreamed through at the
same time in the *Passagenwerk*, like the celebrated analyses of these
commercial arcades or "passages" triggered by capitalistic economy
which ended up creating this bewildering Moebius strip on the
streets of Paris, a space in which the interior is an exterior and conversely, with the attendant litany of objects displayed in the little
shops, or the well-known allegorization of the observer as poet and
flâneur, belongs to an almost childish regression, to wonder in front
of a lost world that has to be reconstituted in all its translucent
details at any cost. This was perceived by Adorno as ahistorical and
magical thinking, the mimetic capture of a lost world that was not
dialectical enough, as a deep-seated fascination for *realia* bordering
on naive materialism. Benjamin's method would send us back to
the associative logic of earlier times when thought processes were
based on natural resemblances between elements or "signatures" of
the world, missing the actual processes of production and the transformations of the bourgeois world by which nineteenth-century
capitalism was characterized. Theory is called upon to provide an
intellectual justification that would be lacking in Benjamin's project
since it was thought to be totally immanent to the very montage
of documents, thoughts, objects, and quotes in which History
consists, insists, and takes shape:

> The direct inference from the duty on wine to *L'Ame du Vin*
> imputes to phenomena precisely the kind of spontaneity, tan-
> gibility and density which they have lost under capitalism. This
> sort of immediate – and I would almost say again "anthro-
> pological" – materialism harbours a profoundly romantic
> element, and the more abruptly and crudely you confront the
> Baudelairean world of forms with the harsh necessities of life,
> the more clearly I detect it. The 'mediation' which I miss and
> find obscured by materialistic–historiographical evocation, is
> simply the theory which your study has omitted. But the
> omission of theory affects the empirical material itself. On the

one hand, this omission lends the material a deceptively epic character, and on the other it deprives the phenomena, which are experienced merely subjectively, of their real historico-philosophical weight.[19]

In an attitude which calls up the frustration and condemnation expressed by Marx and Engels facing the undialectical nature of Max Stirner's thoughts on the Unique's lack of substance coupled with a defiant assertion of "property" in *The German Ideology*, Adorno hits at the religious remainder in Benjamin, the root of what he perceives as anti-theoretical. Magic has to be dispelled like a vapor still clinging to mystified "facts": "If one wanted to put it rather drastically, one could say that your study is located at the crossroads of magic and positivism. This spot is bewitched. Only theory could break this spell – your own resolute and salutary speculative theory. It is simply the claim of this theory that I bring against you here."[20]

It would be very misleading to think that Adorno just requests more Marxism from Benjamin – in fact he wants less Marxism, since he believes that Benjamin is doing violence to his own theoretical self by an excessive respect for materialism: this deluded Marxism betrays, however, a lack of concern for social process and progress. As he writes a little later in the same letter, if there is only one truth, Benjamin is intelligent enough to seize it or convey it – he should not stand in awe of an imaginary party line which would prevent him from leaving his enchanted arcades:

> God knows, there is only one truth, and if your powers of intelligence can seize this one truth through categories which may seem apocryphal to you given your conception of materialism, then you will capture more of this one truth than you will ever do by employing conceptual tools that merely resist your grip at every turn. After all, there is more of this one truth in Nietzsche's Genealogy of Morals than in Bukharin's ABC of Communism.[21]

However, the letter finishes with a list of reasons why the Institute cannot print Benjamin's manuscript as it is, which will force him to revise, water-down the analysis in parts and cut, and finally send only the materials for the Baudelaire book to his friends. For the sake of brevity, I cannot comment here on Benjamin's wonderful response to Adorno, a response that does not yield an inch of ground and rather asserts that the theory is there, although not spelled out or explicit. When Adorno pretends not to understand the deep necessity of the *flâneur* motif, Benjamin replies by pointing out the link between his theory about "empathy with the soul of commodity" and Adorno's theory about "the consumption of exchange-value."[22] Indeed, facing this deliberate misreading, he feels as if "the ground were giving way beneath me." The question now arises: how much of this is based upon a misreading? It is true that there is in Benjamin a tendency to replace expositions of historical developments with enumerations of things or facts, or to bypass theoretical interpretation of social mechanisms with a poetic or religious reverence for names (as Adorno puts it: "the theological motif of calling things by their names tends to switch into the wide-eyed presentation of mere facts").[23] This, however, Benjamin replies, is the "proper philological attitude" which may well remain caught up between magic and positivism but will ultimately reach some illumination from the very hesitation: "the philological interpretation of the author should be preserved and overcome in the Hegelian manner by the dialectical materialist. Philology consists in an examination of texts which proceeds by details and thus magically fixates the reader on it."[24] Benjamin is aware of his need to overcome or criticize pure German philology (and here Nietzsche provides a common model for him and Adorno, since he would constantly refer to himself as a "philologist" while stressing inherent ethical limitations in this specialized training), but this will entail both a critique of myth and considerations for what he calls after Baudelaire "modernity" – a term that he refuses to equate with Adorno's notion of "progress."

Given the unfinished status of the *Arcades Project* it would be rash to defend Benjamin's effort on the strength of his readings of, say, Baudelaire. What can be noted is that Adorno's critique manages to be wrong precisely by being "right," that is, missing the real novelty in Benjamin's abruptly imagistic mode of presentation by insisting on Theory. As Jameson has observed, the same remark could apply to the Institute's reaction to Benjamin's groundbreaking essay on "The Work of Art in the Age of its Technological Reproductibility." Noting how the essay had been edited when printed in the *Zeitschrift für Sozialforschung* in 1936, with the omission of words like "Fascism" and "Communism," Jameson shows not only the influence of a tactical discretion given the Institute's relocation in America, but also a wish to use dialectical theory to hone or streamline the rough edges of Benjamin's texts.[25] The notion of "aura" which remains so problematic and has triggered such a long debate in contemporary aesthetics is countered in Benjamin's thesis by the progressive power of a new art that has accepted technology and therefore renounced the old originality, mystical value, and bourgeois fetishization. This implies trusting Russian filmmakers or American popular culture with a revolutionary function they can never possess in Adorno's eyes (Adorno often uses his experience of hearing people laugh in movie theaters to stress that workers are not necessarily better off than the bourgeois). Chaplin and jazz may have more positive effects than Leni Riefenstahl on the one hand, the Hollywood star system on the other; they should not be romanticized as a key to a new humanity characterized by a pervasive "distraction," thus as devoid of bourgeois interiority as possible. Besides, Adorno is totally right when he notes first that the mechanical reproduction of art pieces did not begin with photography in the nineteenth century and then that the same technology underlies both fascist and communist art. I will return to the issue of technology later, noting here as Jameson does a curious evasion of the real history of technology in Benjamin's and Adorno's exchanges.[26]

The point is not to distribute credits or count winning shots. My general contention is that even when Benjamin is "wrong," he always hits something because of the suggestive power of his "dialectical images," whereas when Adorno is "right," which is often the case, he tends to be glib or self-defeating. What I mean by this is quite visible in his 1933 book on Kierkegaard, a book in which Adorno relies on quite a few concepts taken from Benjamin's texts ("baroque thinking," "allegory," and "dialectical image" being the main borrowings). Adorno's central thesis, if one may sum up a book whose baroque style and philosophical complexity are redoubtable, is to show how Kierkegaard is more Hegelian than he thinks. By focusing on the constitution of the aesthetic as a separate domain, he proves quite conclusively that Kierkegaard merely expands Hegel's system in the direction of concreteness and immediacy. Kierkegaard would embody a transitional stage on the way to a critical theory that would take material aesthetics as main object and more rigorous concept. Here is a typical sentence about intuition: "The Hegelian school – to which Kierkegaard owed his material aesthetics as well as the category of totality – was able to give a better account of the centers of aesthetic intuition."[27] The problem is then why should one take Kierkegaard as an important thinker at all if his "truth" has already been provided by Hegel or Marx? The only answer to that question is obviously that behind Kierkegaard one will find Benjamin's particular type of material dialectics of immediacy. What we see in the Kierkegaard book is Adorno settling his accounts with his older friend and some time mentor in advance of their full discussion.

When Adorno describes how Kierkegaard's concept of the inner self is constituted in a dialogue of the philosopher with himself and finally depends upon his having spent too much time talking to his mirror in a bourgeois salon, he is using categories borrowed from Benjamin's essays on Baudelaire and the *flâneur*. "Thus the *flâneur* promenades in his room; the world only appears to him reflected by pure inwardness."[28] But when he delves deeper into the philosophy of immanence and "situations," it is to show how immanence refers to a momentary suspension abolishing the opposition between the subject and the object. This brief moment of indifference (or reification) requires then a myth or a nature to simply last or take a body. In his confused Christian mysticism, Kierkegaard would have anticipated Benjamin's articulation of myth, image, and dialectic.

> Dialectic comes to a stop in the image and cites the mythical in the historically most recent as the distant past: nature as proto-history. For this reason the image, which like those of the *intérieur* brings dialectic and myth to the point of indifferenciation, are truly "antediluvian fossils." They may be called dialectical images, to use Benjamin's expression, whose

63

compelling definition of "allegory" also holds true for Kierkegaard's allegorical intention as a configuration of historical dialectic and mythical nature.[29]

What is fascinating is to see this same passage quoted literally by Benjamin in the *Arcades Project*, without any commentary (although a commentary is announced).[30] This passage was to be inserted in a section devoted to "Refuse of History." In the context, no further commentary was indeed needed.

In a critical assessment of the many recent translations of Benjamin's works into English, J. M. Coetzee seems to agree with Adorno in his ironic and distanced evaluation facing the current Benjamin cult. He notes how difficult it is to situate Benjamin, neither a gifted story-teller nor a professional critic or philosopher, not really a historian either (this was the reason why his thesis was never accepted by the German university).[31] It would be too simple or dismissive to present him as a dreamer or *flâneur* of Theory. The lack of precise domain or a specific competence is nevertheless constitutive of Theory, and it is also emblematic of the broad movement in the arts and letters we call "modernism." Benjamin is indispensable for Theory precisely because his central obsession was to define modernity (a modernity that is not without its shadowy double of nostalgia) without having to believe in the myth of Progress as Adorno did in the name of Marxism. Coetzee, who happens to be a remarkable novelist, is in a good position (and at times, quite unsparing) in denouncing Benjamin's hopeless contradictions, which leads him to compare the German writer with an American contemporary more and more often quoted alongside his work, Ezra Pound. For, even if Coetzee does not say so, the famous "theory" Adorno was missing in the *Arcades* book can easily be equated with what Ezra Pound used to call the "ideogrammic method." This method of poetic composition consisted in the juxtaposition of vivid particulars or splintered images whose assemblage would then evoke a concept in the mind of the reader or beholder. Even if the analogy with Chinese characters has no philological validity (no ideogram is composed of pictorial representations of simple objects which once put together illustrate an idea, as Fenollosa had claimed), this mythical and grammatological foundation would not be without echoing with Benjamin's main idea that all sorts of "traces" are to be seen in material objects and that these lead the reader like a detective to the comprehension of what always appears as the scene of a crime. As Benjamin would repeat to Adorno: "The concept of the trace is defined and determined philosophically in opposition to the concept of the aura."[32]

> From a distance, Benjamin's magnum opus is curiously reminiscent of another great ruin of twentieth-century literature, Ezra Pound's Cantos. Both are the issue of years of jackdaw reading. Both are built out of fragments and quotations, and adhere to the high-modernist aesthetics of image and montage. Both have economic ambitions and economists are presiding figures (Marx in one case, Gesell and Douglas in the other). Both authors have investments in antiquarian bodies of knowledge whose relevance to their own times they overestimate. Neither knows when to stop. And both were in the end consumed by the monster of fascism, Benjamin tragically, Pound shamefully.[33]

Coetzee's comparison "illuminates" (to use a verb Benjamin liked) because it situates the mysticism of Theory and the resistance to Theory – both movements being at work with equal momentum in Benjamin – in the context of a tragic modernism. What is perhaps more revealing is the growing impact of Benjamin's thought on the rapidly expanding field of modernist studies; I cannot count the number of recent presentations or books in progress devoted to "Joyce and Benjamin," "Benjamin and Aragon," or "Pound and Benjamin." As Coetzee suggests, we will soon have, next to maps of Dublin in 1904 (so as to visit *Ulysses* more comfortably) compendiums and tourist guides to the *Arcades Project* – but that will not be a bad thing.

Responding Dialogically

There could not be arcades in Bakhtin's works – one needs to hear the winds blowing freely on a landscape of steppes. Besides, one cannot imagine what map would help one visit Bakhtin's *oeuvre*; it would surely have to be a "chronotope," both intimately connected to the particularities of time and place (revolutionary fervor replaced by Stalinist terror and the like) and deploying itself in the verticality of time from post-revolutionary Russia to the dawn of European culture. At one level, Bakhtin's long and complex career could make him the perfect anti-Kojève. The two Russian thinkers began their training by reading the same books at the same time, threading an original way between dominant neo-Kantism and emerging Husserlian phenomenology. However, while Kojève chose Hegel as a strategic stronghold to occupy, from which he would make inroads into Marx and Heidegger, Bakhtin opted for a more fluid position, an open attitude in which literature and ethics played an equal role and epistemological hysteria was replaced by meek yet stubborn resistance to ideological coercion, while sweeping claims to absolute knowledge were undermined by an endlessly incomplete dialogism. A further irony was that a declared Stalinist like Kojève completed a brilliant administrative career in France while Bahktin kept dodging prison, exile, and repression in Stalinist Russia before being rehabilitated when de-Stalinization had run full course. Whereas Kojève was pleased to play the master explaining another master to an untrained audience, Bakhtin was content to live in semi-obscurity and let his friends sign his books or articles.

In fact, no other phrase applies to Bakhtin better than Charcot's famous quip to Freud: "La théorie, c'est bon, mais cela n'empêche pas d'exister" – a sentence which starts in a suspended lilt like a demi-alexandrine cut by two commas before hurrying to meet common sense, and which could be roughly translated as: "Theory is fine and all, but it does not prevent us/things from existing." One finds this in Freud's obituary written as homage to his master in hysteria, Charcot. Freud's account in the 1893 obituary leaves unnamed the identity of the German students who were raising objections to Charcot's empirical methods. One (evidently Freud, as an earlier version of the text makes clear)[34] blurted out: "This cannot possibly be, it contradicts the theory of Young–Helmholtz," to which Charcot replied the well-known utterance. "[Charcot] did not reply, 'So much the worse for theory, clinical facts rank first,' and so forth. But he did say – leaving us deeply impressed 'La théorie, c'est bon, mais cela n'empêche pas d'exister.'" What obviously impressed Freud was the master's ironical equanimity, his refusal of a staunch defense of either the experimental method based on observation leading to a therapy that did not shrink before trials and errors, or a dogmatic, i.e., "German," method based on deduction from *a priori* theories. Charcot's rejoinder is particularly felicitous as it both hints at a return to "things themselves" in clinical practice (symptoms will keep baffling scientists in spite of their nice theories) or at quasi-existentialist resilience (we may have our pet theories but we are only human after all, and just give me a break Dr. Freud). After all, theory may be "good," but something else is needed to reach a correct diagnosis and enjoy life at the same time. Theory is the foreign specter of abstract totalization speaking in a strange accent, while "we" locals know how to live fully.

The double theme contained in "does not prevent from existing" runs though all of Bakhtin's early notebooks. I will take a look at fragments from an untitled treatise devoted to a "first philosophy" in the making. They were written in 1919–21 and were only salvaged half a century later, from a storeroom in which they were slowly being eaten by rats. They correspond to the first phase in the philosopher's career, when he was dialoguing with Kant, Nietzsche, Hermann Cohen, Bergson, and Husserl in an effort to elaborate an original doctrine of "responsibility" or "answerability." Bakhtin's main enemy is what he calls "theoreticism," a broad term which includes Platonism, Kant's formalism, psychologism, and positivism. He also carefully distinguishes his position from that of vitalism, be it either Dilthey's or Bergson's, in the name of an ethical philosophy which seems to announce with uncanny precision the ethical critique of metaphysics launched by Levinas. Bakhtin defends an embodied thinking linked to the novelty of the here and now, a position he calls "participative thinking" (*uchastnoe myshlenie*), which calls up all at once commitment, engagement, or a doctrine of non-indifference. In a brilliant phrase he defines this as "my non-alibi in Being"[35] – my "being now and there" anticipates Heidegger's *Dasein* but inserts it from the start into a network of moral connections; there is no alibi that could relieve me of my responsibility for my acts, I am not elsewhere in the name of an abstract law. The "performative" (*postupochnaia*) fullness of the affirmation of one's being-there-and-now entails an "act" that will be both uniquely mine and universalizable. Singularity and irreplaceability do not exclude a consideration for the other; like Max Stirner's "Unique" who is compelled to posit a community of egoists, Bakhtin's singular ego is already shot through with alterity. "I" is indissociable from "the other" and the "I–for-the-other."[36]

Bakhtin's philosophy of the answerable act seems very close to what a novelist like Hermann Broch would try to systematize a few years later, especially in the philosophical sections of the *Sleepwalkers* (a novel to which I will return in chapter 4), by elaborating a theory of the subjective positioning of values that is nevertheless part of an "architectonic" construction in which the ethical and aesthetic worlds bleed into each other endlessly. For Broch as for Bakhtin, "theory" as such is to be rejected when it loses touch with the subjective pole of the act:

> The theoretical and aesthetic worlds have been set at liberty, but from within these worlds themselves it is impossible to connect them and bring them into communion with the ultimate unity, i.e., to incarnate them. Since theory has broken away from the actually performed act and develops according to its own immanent law, the performed act itself, having released theory from itself, begins to deteriorate. All the energy of answerable performing is drawn off into the autonomous domain of culture . . . Theory consigns the performed act or deed to the realm of brute being, drains it of all the moments of ideality in it and draws them into its own autonomous self-contained domain, that is, totally impoverishes the actually performed act. This is the source from which Tolstoyism and all forms of cultural nihilism draw their impelling inspiration.[37]

Here is the root of Bakhtin's demonization of Tolstoy and praise for Dostoevsky: Tolstoy's historical syntheses and compelling narratives may be aesthetically perfect, but they fail to represent the openness of internal dialogism Bakhtin has discovered in life and in Dostoevsky's novels. Already in the 1919–21 notebook, Tolstoy represents a "monologism" even if the term is not yet coined, and if Dostoevsky is not mentioned, it falls to Pushkin to embody the values of a double center of consciousness. It is quite telling that the first part of the treatise that was to deal with the architectonic of the act consists in fact of a long commentary on a lyrical poem, "Parting." This Romantic poem written in 1830 could not be considered "dialogical" in the more experimental sense of the term, since it just describes how the hero says a passionate goodbye to a beloved about to return to the southern shores of Italy. As if to prove the interpenetration of philosophy and literature, Bakhtin needs to engage in a detailed paraphrase and analysis of the poem to test the principle of "an architectonic interrelationship of two valuatively affirmed *others*."[38] It is finally aesthetic contemplation in itself which is defined as refering "an object to the valuative plane of the *other*."[39] As with Levinas's meditation on literature (strongly influenced by Dostoevsky too) there is no clear demarcation between ethics and aesthetics.

The 1919–21 notebooks contain the seeds of all the later books, including a rather misguided attack on psychoanalysis considered as tainted by biological determinism and an ambivalent praise of Marxism, which "in spite of its defects" allows for the concrete building of performances in actually historical contexts.[40] They show the fecundity and the limitations of the philosophy of the act, which are nowhere more apparent than in the first version of the Dostoevsky book. The tragic irony is that *Problems of Dostoevsky's Art* was published in May 1929 just months after Bakhtin's arrest earlier that year.[41] This book, the first actually signed by Bakhtin, may have been instrumental in reducing his sentence to exile to Kazakhstan. Despite courageous efforts by competent critics like David Lodge and Lynne Pearce,[42] Bakhtin's thesis rests on an untenable hypothesis: Dostoevsky would write as if he did not know what his characters were going to say, as if they were absolutely free. It would be easy to demonstrate that dialogism is merely an impression left on a sensitive reader interested above all in the ideological or religious issues debated on stage, as it were, that the characters speak here and there next to the author. What is remarkable is the claim made in the name of Dostoevsky: the new novel goes back to Dante as soon as it is polyphonic, that is, determined throughout by interaction and conflict in such a way that it never ends but is open onto an eschatological or messianic future. The conception of polyphony elaborated here is not stylistic; Bakhtin is able to describe how a short story by Tolstoy, "Three Deaths," in which class differences correspond to different levels in tone and style, is monologic, while Dostoevsky's characters, who all speak more or less in the same way, embody heteroglossia and multi-voicedness.[43] What matters therefore is content (Tolstoy describes three deaths, whereas Dostoevsky prefers moments of crisis, thresholds before a decision) and the handling of subjectivity.

It would be wrong to think that this unqualified praise for one writer and blindness facing another can be blamed on youthful enthusiasm for the issues at hand, for it is quite surprising to see an older and mature thinker restate exactly the same thesis; one of the later pieces has this passage: "In Dostoevsky, where the characters are ideologists, the author and such heroes (thinker-ideologists) end up on the same plane. The dialogic context and situations of the speeches of the characters differ essentially from those of the authorial speech."[44] The only polyphonic novel would thus be Flann O'Brien's *At Swim-Two-Birds*, since it narrates the revolt of the characters against their author! What remains in this philosophical approach to literary semantics is the powerful and empowering insight that each text is made up of conflicting voices, often opposing an "authoritative discourse" (the discourse of official ideology which cannot stand any dissenting opinion) and an "internally persuasive discourse" through which new evaluations can emerge until alterity be recognized as such.

This insight was developed in the monumental thesis devoted to Rabelais, a thesis which Bakhtin had completed in 1946 but which was only ratified by academic authorities in 1952. There his genius appears in full light: the idea that Rabelais's work makes more sense when replaced in the context of a history of popular laughter, defined by an insistence on the low, the scatological, and the obscene, in a carnivalesque inversion of all higher values, still keeps some of the Romanticism of a pure "folk" but is caught up in an irresistible movement of affirmation and resistance to oppression. Bakhtin's amazing culture allows him to take into account Greek, Roman, and Hellenistic novels and then find submerged patterns reactivated in the Middle Ages. Despite his rather conventional tastes and his avoidance of avant-garde writers (his latest notebooks condemn Joyce and Proust as monologists, which is not totally surprising), Bakhtin not only links his investigations to a very broad historiography of popular culture still in the making, but also provides a much needed philosophical authority to emerging new historicisms and cultural studies. Bakhtin's main legacy to Kristeva was his pioneering analysis of intertextuality, a term that has become standard in literary criticism today,[45] as well as his double stress on a material tradition and open-ended texts, which corresponds with the more recent turn to textual studies of drafts and manuscripts, and to the whole school of "genetic criticism" that I will introduce later. Bakhtin's influence on Barthes, for one, was crucial, since it corresponded to his progressive disillusionment with purely scientific models. As this influence was mediated by Julia Kristeva and the seminars of Barthes of the *Tel Quel* discussion groups, I will have to explore at length the specific context in which the transformation occurred.

The Invention of "Writing"

The central role I have ascribed to Barthes in the last century's fascination for High Theory is easy to demonstrate. A colleague of mine told me how Barthes, occasionally invited as a visiting professor to Johns Hopkins University, was shown the neighboring University of Pennsylvania library with all its archives and treasures. Obviously impressed, Barthes declared that he would never have written any book if he had had such a research facility at his disposal. This is not so flippant as it may sound, and gives a not-too-fanciful image of Barthes, reading slowly, by himself, refusing scholarly guides or indexes, patiently chewing away through Michelet's collected works, exactly as he pictured Michelet devouring centuries in his historiographical recreations. On the other hand, history and literature would always be thoroughly digested into well formulated ideas, and thus Barthes is the exact opposite of very learned critics like George Steiner, who are so eager to display the extent of their erudition that one finishes their books still wondering what the thesis was.

In my historical sketch of a hystericized and hystericizing Theory,

I have taken the Barthes of 1953 as a point of departure, purposely eliding another moment, say New York in 1942, when the community of exiles numbered André Breton, Claude Lévi-Strauss, and Roman Jakobson. The collaboration of Jakobson and Lévi-Strauss did launch the "linguistic moment" which was to reverberate so momentously, exerting lasting effects on Barthes himself. I have suggested that *Writing Degree Zero* was a better point of departure, a lever for Theory because I take the title very literally, and assume that even if the book does not aim at providing an absolute beginning (what other beginning would there be than Plato, Aristotle, or Heraclitus?), its title parades a zero moment, laying theoretical foundations, positing itself at the outset of a revolution which, in Marx's phrase, revisits the tragedies of ancient times by turning them into farce. Thus farce and seriousness were both enacted by Barthes when he started his book by going back, quite purposefully, to key idioms of the French Revolution. Let us examine the opening gambit of his book by comparing the original and the translation.

This is how *Writing Degree Zero* begins in Lavers's and Smith's translation:

> Hébert, the revolutionary, never began a number of his news-sheet *Le Père Duchêne* without introducing a sprinkling of obscenities. These improprieties had no real meaning, but they had significance. In what way? In that they expressed a whole revolutionary situation. Now here is an example of a mode of writing whose function is no longer only communication or expression, but the imposition of something beyond language, which is both History and the stand we take in it.
>
> It is impossible to write without labeling oneself: as with *Le Père Duchêne*, so equally with Literature.[46]

Here, just to have a taste of Barthes's style, is the French original:

> Hébert ne commençait jamais un numéro du *Père Duchêne* sans y mettre quelques "foutre" et quelques "bougre." Ces grossièretés ne signifiaient rien mais elles signalaient. Quoi? Toute une situation révolutionnaire. Voilà donc l'exemple d'une écriture dont la fonction n'est pas seulement de com-

muniquer ou d'exprimer, mais d'imposer un au-delà du langage qui est à la fois l'Histoire et le parti qu'on y prend.

Il n'y a pas de langage écrit sans affiche, et ce qui est vrai du *Père Duchêne*, l'est également de la Littérature.[47]

A purposely over-literal translation would look like this:

Hébert never began a number of *Le Père Duchêne* without introducing a few "fucks" and "buggers." These obscenities did not signify but they signaled. What? A whole revolutionary situation. Here is therefore an example of a writing whose function is not just to communicate or to express, but to impose a beyond of language, which is both History and the stand one takes in it.

There is no written language that does not flaunt its signals, thus what is true of *Le Père Duchêne* is equally true of Literature.

My aim is not to discredit a competent though dated translation (it was done in 1967), but to show how the wish to explain as well as translate an essay that aims at the status of pamphlet can weaken its force and distort its theoretical stakes. Barthes begins by displaying quickly garish stylistic markers, and it is inevitable to find equivalents for them – even if I am guilty of some over-translation, since the terms "fuck" and "bugger," while correct, had a different ring in 1790, and one should take a look at their frequent use in Sade's works for instance. To give another example, it is as if Barthes had quoted the opening of Jarry's *Père Ubu* (and there's not a little of Père Duchêne in Père Ubu!) and taken its resounding first "Merdre!" as a paradigm of *writing*. Of course, Barthes assumes an audience responsive to French history and able to situate correctly Hébert in his context – one can imagine American students asking: Hébert the revolutionary? Which revolution? This shows the dynamic function of the linguistic example in the launching of a problematic which entails conceptual distinctions (between "to signify" and "to signal," for instance) and also forces its readers to feel "embarked," to use Pascal's term, that is, implied in a historical situation: there choices will have to be made all the time and willy-nilly, consciously or unconsciously. By dramatizing two "beginnings" (the zesty rhetorical openings of the *Père Hébert* and the new departure embodied by the regicide and "noblicide" politics of the most radical factions of the French Revolution) Barthes skillfully splices History and Textuality, both linked through a "writing" taken as a springboard for his own demonstration. Any language that will be subsequently seen as aspiring to a similar "zero degree" will somehow tend to recapture this revolutionary fervor, the ethical transparency of absolute beginnings.

Moreover, the term *écriture* is introduced here without great fanfare, following imperceptibly from the examples: we will agree immediately that peppering one's political pamphlets with "bugger!" not only introduces ruptures typical of spoken style that jar with the formal constraints of written style, but also manifests a desire to shock or awaken the audience. What is more startling is that we find ourselves having accepted the idea that such a process is not exceptional, restricted to times of upheaval or crises like the French Revolution, but is in fact emblematic of Literature as such – and we have reached that point by the beginning of the second paragraph! Do we then need the long and pedantic footnote appended to the first occurrence of the term *writing* in the English version? The translators send us to Barthes's own *Elements of Semiology* so as to stress that "writing" in Barthes's text is not limited to "handwriting" or to "the art of writing" but includes all the meanings conveyed by the verb *écrire* in French. They add: "It is used here in a strictly technical sense to denote a new concept, and is translated as 'writing,' 'mode of writing.'"[48] I do not see what has been gained by translating *écriture* as "mode of writing" in this introduction; I would rather insist on the apparent non-technicality of the term, which is slipped under our feet as it were to gain our assent, and is only later introduced conceptually, in the definitions provided by the first chapter. What is worse, the footnote refers the definition of this new concept of "writing" back to the term "idiolect," which is developed, it is true, in *Elements of Semiology* I.1.6 and I.1.7. Alas, if one takes a closer look at the passage in question, it becomes quite clear that with the idea of an idiolect, Barthes launches into a comprehensive discussion of "style" and not at all of "writing"!

One has to turn to the groundbreaking terminological distinc-

tions offered in the first chapter of *Writing Degree Zero* to understand how Barthes's poetics supposes an interaction between several
main terms: "literature" is seen as the history of the evolution of
forms, "language" is akin to an element, a social medium granted
to all speakers and whose evolution is so slow that it is barely perceptible by individual users, and "style," is understood as a writer's
singularity, the specificity of biographical constraints similar to the
inescapable fate provided by one's body.[49] On Barthes's view, only
"writing" will provide the space of historicity and freedom that can
wedge itself between biographical determinations (like the links
between Proust's asthma and his long sentences) and the socio-
cultural negotiations between language and literature.

> A language and a style are blind forces; a mode of writing [*écri-
> ture*] is an act of historical solidarity. A language and a style are
> objects; a mode of writing is a function: it is the relationship
> between creation and society, the literary language transformed
> by its social finality, form considered as a human intention and
> thus linked to the great crises of History. . . . Placed at the
> center of the problematics of literature, which cannot exist
> prior to it, writing is thus essentially the morality of form, the
> choice of that social area within which the writer elects to
> situate the Nature of his language.[50]

What stands out in an uncanny way is how much Barthes's discourse is modeled after Sartre's own dialectics of freedom and determination, commitment and historical responsibility. It is well known
that the first installments of *Writing Degree Zero* in *Combat* were
published in 1947, just months after Sartre's *What is Literature?* had
been published. Barthes's first chapter "What is Writing?" quotes
Sartre's first chapter while inverting its main terms. Whereas Sartre
defined writing in terms of communication and collective responses
to a historical situation, Barthes wrenches the term from Sartre's
humanistic and neo-Marxist dialectics and endows it with a totally
different function: writing negotiates endlessly but freely between
two human formations which are taken as if they were "natures,"
language and style. Sartre needed the articulation of two terms for
his dialectics, "language" and "style": language is determined by

communication, while style is seen as means of expression. Sartre comes perilously close to returning to a dialectics of form and content, or an even grosser opposition between private speech and collective discourses. By providing three terms, Barthes moves out of this conceptual vice. *Écriture* will be emancipated from a forced dilemma in which one had to choose between a private discourse, often the production of a small coterie who will be necessarily obscure and apolitical (one can think of Mallarmé, clearly not a model for Sartre then), and socially responsible positions leading to the role of the committed intellectual on the lookout for generous causes and critical denunciations.

The term *writing* will accrue to itself all the features traditionally attributed to *style* while eschewing the formalist or evaluative overtones of stylistics. By defining writing as the "morality of form," Barthes lends a moral and even political weight to purely formal inventions. The main lever for Theory was thus ready for use in 1953. One can note that Barthes's new usage makes sense above all in a French history of modernity going from Flaubert and Mallarmé to the *Nouveau Roman*, and bypasses the possibility of understanding the plural of "styles" in a historicized way, half-way between individual agents and collective formations, as most modernists like Joyce, Eliot, and Pound would have it. What was lost for stylistics was gained at the level of a History of Writing: through this new practice of writing, language and literature will be made to interact productively and even create revolutionary assemblages. From a consideration of what is undeniably "historical writing" (Hébert's pamphlets) we have moved to the momentous assertion that "History is a writing."[51]

The story of how Barthes had not only to fight his way out of Sartre's neo-Hegelian dialectics but also wrestle with the objections of academics like Professor Picard, who ended up embodying what was dead (even when they were "right" in terms of pure scholarship) in the Sorbonne, has often been told. No doubt, Barthes's success was helped by his having found other bases than traditional academia, be they the École Pratique des Hautes Études en Sciences Sociales or the little magazines of the literary avant-garde. This will lead us to discussion of how another medium could embody both the spirit of the avant-garde and a Theory armed with the concept of the history of Writing. To conclude on what I take as the founding moment of Theory in 1953 via the introduction of the concept *writing*, I cannot help observing how subtle suggestions of hysteria or terror would reintroduce Hegelian motives at the same time as they were discarded. This was also Paulhan's main objection in *Les Fleurs de Tarbes* to which Blanchot had answered in *La Part du feu*. Leaving this discussion aside for the moment, I will focus on the theoretical moment embodied by *Tel Quel*, a review whose theories owed as much to Barthes as to Blanchot. In fact, Blanchot was deliberately spurned by the *Tel Quelians* as a contemporary reference or ignored as a precursor, precisely because his theses were thought to be too Hegelian, which meant for them too idealist.[52] Terror and hysteria will then be the main unspoken symptoms lurking behind strategies of the avant-garde deployed by *Tel Quel*.

Theory and/or the Avant-Garde

For two decades the review *Tel Quel* managed to be more than a periodical: between 1960 and 1982 it promoted a sophisticated French avant-garde open to international modernism, in a replay of the dilemmas opposing modernism and the avant-garde as Peter Bürger has shown. If it fell short of launching a political movement, the review embodied, summed up, or allegorized a whole state of mind; in short, stood for what is now seen with nostalgia and awe as "the age of Theory." Its deployment of typically avant-garde shock tactics, terroristic denunciations, and political contestation never hampered its constant amassing of cultural capital and its feedback toward a larger tradition. In order to avoid sociological reductionism[53] or hagiography glossing over staggering palinodies,[54] a historical perspective should yield a fresh understanding of what has been at stake in the link established by *Tel Quel* between the cultural politics of the avant-garde, the wish to take literary production in consideration, and the promotion of a new "science" of signs, writing, and textuality. Theory could not thrive without these three elements and they were all promoted by the members of *Tel Quel*. The review also provides a number of critical markers with which one can gauge theory's impact on Anglo-Saxon audiences (via the relay of British reviews like *Screen*) and explains the depth and speed of the subsequent general rejection.

It is crucial to resist biographical readings or the temptation to reduce *Tel Quel* to a tool cleverly used by literary *arrivistes* like Sollers or Kristeva. Although Sollers dominated the periodical, being the only founding member who always figured on the editorial board, the review's rise to fame, its extreme contradictions, and surprisingly rapid collapse should be seen as historical and cultural symptoms, compromise formations that condense an entire *Zeitgeist*. Philippe Joyaux (his real name) consciously strove after literary models: a Joycean identification was followed by mimetic reenactments of Céline, the two forebears finally meeting in the writing of *Paradis*. Radical literary experimentations like Joyce's or Artaud's would typically embody a site of resistance, the best antidote against fascism and middle-class complacency. Sollers arranged to his advantage the editorial power games that gave a stamp to the review; meanwhile the history of the magazine gathered speed as it reflected more and more adequately the acceleration of real history in France in the watershed years just before and after May 1968.

Tel Quel was launched by Le Seuil, a press known for its left-wing Catholic sympathies and its interest in promoting the budding market for human sciences. The two main personalities who presided over the birth of the magazine were Jean-Hedern Hallier and Sollers. Hallier was soon to fight with his partners and to discredit himself in dubious political ventures. Uniting these young talents was a friendship with an older writer, a poet essentially, Francis Ponge, still relatively unknown at that time. To distinguish itself from the *nouveau roman* school, the main claim to originality in the first issues of *Tel Quel* was its constant reference to the works of Ponge, whose texts are now seen as having dominated French poetry and poetics after World War II, but who was clearly extremely isolated then. A fruitful alliance between an older and half-recognized poet and a bunch of enthusiastic young men lent *Tel Quel* its initial impetus.

Besides, the name of the review calls up another poet, Paul Valéry, who had chosen this title when he reprinted "as such" critical jottings and reflections just a few years before he died.[55] Valéry's importance cannot be exaggerated: he was the single French writer of importance to uphold the notion of literary theory in the first half of the twentieth century, and his obstinacy in denying authorial intention (he would often say that his poetry had only the meaning provided by his readers) and stressing the intellectual or reflexive element in literature made him a very apt model. Besides, Valéry occupied the chair of Poetics at the Collège de France from 1937 to his death in 1945. This chair was founded for him, and in his inaugural speech Valéry had to justify the need for a study of poetics whose object would be "the positive phenomenon of production and consumption in the realm of intellectual works,"[56] an object that could not be encompassed by literary history alone. Valéry's main principle was the following: "Literature is, and cannot be anything but, the extension and application of certain properties of language,"[57] a principle which also underwrote Russian Formalism and American New Criticism. To launch what he already called a "theory of literature" investigating "effects that can be called properly literary" without spurning the study of manuscripts, Valéry gave the name of "Poetics."[58] True to this program, all the entries in Valéry's *Tel Quel* that pertain to literature insist upon the technical aspect of the craft: "What a shame to write without knowing what language, verb, metaphors, idea shifts, tone shifts are; without knowing the *structure* of the work's duration or the conditions of its closure; knowing barely why and not even how!"[59]

Valéry reopens a dialogue with Aristotle which had been lost in French culture since Racine, if one excepts a neo-Thomism that was briefly fashionable from the last decades of the nineteenth century to the 1920s with Jacques Maritain but had more impact on writers like David Jones or James Joyce. Valéry stresses that the etymology of *Poetic* implies any kind of creative activity, including practical activities, scientific inventions and, in the case of poetry, its revisions and various drafts. Valéry could be compared with poets like Eliot and Pound and seen in a wider modernism always intent upon bridging the gap between literary experimentation and literary reflection. A distinction made both in the Collège de France lecture and in *Tel Quel* will have important consequences: it is the distinction between works that are created by their audience and works that create their audiences.[60] Clearly, Sollers and

friends chose the second alternative. It was with the aim of creating a new audience that the first issue's epigraph quoting the phrase
tel quel came, not from Valéry's title but from a different author,
Nietzsche. The review opened its first issue with an epigraph on
the "eternal return of the same" underwriting a positive and
joyous affirmation of life considered both in itself and as spectacle,
a tension bequeathing a redoubtable hesitation in view of ulterior
developments:

> I want the world and I want it as is (*tel quel*), I want it still, I
> want it eternally, and I cry out, insatiably: encore!, and not
> only for myself but for the whole play and for the whole spec-
> tacle and not only for the whole spectacle but at bottom for
> me, because the spectacle has become necessary, because it
> makes me necessary, because I am necessary to it and I render
> it necessary.[61]

The superbly exalted purple prose of *Beyond Good and Evil*
announces a radical departure from the then dominant notion of a
committed literature. By starting from Nietzsche's most paradoxical
thought, a thought which, as he confessed it himself, would lead
anyone to insanity, the *Tel Quelians* decided to flirt with drama,
madness, despair – or, in the words of Bataille about the eternal
return of the Same: "The Return is the whole man's dramatic mode
and his mask; it is the desert of a man whose every instant is hence-
forward unmotivated."[62]

An atheological "Chance" will accordingly provide the only
rationale for man's behavior, from his writings (think of Mallarmé's
Throw of Dice here) to his most intimate or political decisions. If he
can hardly accommodate Sartre, Nietzsche is after all not incompatible with Valéry, a post-Mallarmean poet who had already paro-
died some of the pretensions and contradictions of a solipsistic
Uebermann in *Monsieur Teste*. Above all, Nietzsche brings through
this perfect epigraph a whiff of hysteria, a definite suggestion of
stylistic panic, along with a neat theoretical double bind: doesn't he
want the world "as is," thus flying in the face of any Romanticism
always tempted to play out the duality of what is flatly given out
there, and of what can be redeemed or saved through the process

of desire, by the imagination of an elsewhere? This wish is postulated and not logically posited, but it will make the subject indispensable to a worldly process ultimately contained in that same exercise of the will. It was also in 1961 that Heidegger denounced Nietzsche's alleged subversion of metaphysics as its very culmination, as its last and wild excrescence marked by the reduction of ontology to a subjectivism of the will. Less a Will-to-Power than a Will-to-Madness, we find here all the trappings of a histrionic parading of excess without which avant-garde bluster would be indistinguishable from the syllabuses of mere teachers of rhetoric. Hysteria, yes, but "as is," or Germanic passion moderated by French taste.

Thus out of the somewhat cacophonic medley of the beginnings, certain choices stand out clearly when one peruses the contents of the first issue: Ponge opens and closes the issue, Camus is paid a very tactical homage, and next to Virginia Woolf, only Jean Cayrol and Claude Simon appear as recognized writers. Ideology is held at some distance, serious literary technique alone seems endowed with an ethical role. In the second number, the discussion of *nouveau roman* continues and in the following issues, the names of Claude Ollier, Robert Pinget, Michel Butor, Nathalie Sarraute, and Louis-René des Forêts recur. Although the links with the *new novel* group became looser, Jean Ricardou, who joined the review in 1962, would later specialize in rigorous examinations of the formal procedures of this school. It is the original endorsement of the formalism of the *new novel* that leads to the first break: one of the founders, Huguenin, was forced to leave *Tel Quel* in June 1960 for embracing a Romanticism condemning the "technological" style of the writerly models chosen by the others. His death in a car accident in 1962 enshrined him in the relatively long list of celebrities who lost their lives on French roads (Camus was another egregious victim).[63] Sollers's second novel, *Le Parc*, was crowned by the Medicis prize in 1961 and seen as a competent imitation of Robbe-Grillet. A general uproar greeted the prize, conservative critics deploring that Sollers should dilapidate his literary gifts and fall under the domination of fashion, while a number of serious writers like Leiris, Gérard Genette, and Louis-René des Forêts insisted that his evolution paved the way for the constitution of a true avant-garde. What was not missed was the review's apparent political neutrality at the time of mounting political protest against the Algerian war. Without dubbing it a "right-wing" review, the early collusion between the *new novel* and *Tel Quel* signals a refusal of explicit political commitment; this was the juvenile *faux pas* that the subsequent radicalization of the group would try to correct.

As new personalities joined the committee like Jean-Louis Baudry, Michel Deguy, Marcelin Pleynet, and Denis Roche, who all questioned the very possibility of literature, or of poetry, at least it increased its avant-garde stance. Roche played with panache the role of a negative poet when he declared that "poetry is inadmissible and besides it does not exist." Two important critics joined the group, Genette and Jean-Pierre Faye, which contributed to the development of a more serious theoretical outlook, and they were relayed by Barthes, who published a number of important essays between 1961 and 1964 in *Tel Quel*. Answers to a general questionnaire on the use and function of criticism were published in the summer of 1963, while the names of Bataille and Ezra Pound, less translated than glossed by Roche, suggested new avenues of literary and philosophical experimentation. By the mid-1960s *Tel Quel* could be seen as a serious, committed, and unrivaled magazine aiming at disseminating the theory and practice of a literary structuralism which looked very much like a revised version of Russian Formalism. The Parisian avant-garde found new bearings when it perceived affinities with the Russian avant-garde that had been active in the 1920s. When Tzvetan Todorov presented the texts of the Russian poets and critics in his *Théorie de la littérature* in 1965, the names of Khlebnikov, Brik, Shklovsky, Jakobson, and Eikhenbaum were news in French circles. Todorov relayed by *Tel Quel* put an end to the obscurity surrounding these authors and when Julia Kristeva arrived upon the scene a year later, soon to be captured by Sollers (who married her), she brought a similar Slavic expertise to the group: coming like Todorov from Bulgaria, she completed the formalist picture by adding new references to the semioticians of the Tartu school and to Mikhail Bakhtin, then almost totally unknown in France. Not only was the history of the avant-garde sanctioned by reference to a previous movement which had established political credentials, a very concrete proof was also given that one could be a "formalist" (that is, interest oneself in exploring the literariness and literality of poetic and novelistic languages) and a revolutionary at the same time. Kristeva nevertheless did not dispel certain ambiguities and allowed some confusion to float. If it was almost impossible at the time to distinguish between Medvedev, Voloshinov, and Bakhtin, Kristeva downplayed Bakhtin's staunch opposition to Formalism.

However, from Todorov's *Théorie de la littérature* to Julia Kristeva's *Séméiotiké* in 1969 (essays previously published in *Tel Quel*), a whole revolution had taken place in the field of literary semiotics, a revolution in which *Tel Quel* had played a key role. When the review devoted a special issue to Antonin Artaud in 1965, it included a groundbreaking essay by a young philosopher, Jacques Derrida. Derrida's impact was immediately felt and his name was called upon more and more frequently in the pages of the review. As we have seen, Derrida introduced another dimension through a philosophical questioning of the main theses underpinning structuralism, while sharing several structuralist tenets, like the Saussurean idea that there are only differences in language. On the other hand, *Tel Quel* provided the philosopher with a tribune, a sounding board, and a series of invitations to engage with literary issues: the essay Derrida devoted to Mallarmé in 1969 came from a "double session" given at the well-attended *Tel Quel* reading group called *Theoretical Study Group*, while the piece entitled "Dissemination" consisted in a jumble of quotations from Sollers's *Nombres*.[64] Derrida identified in *Nombres* the utopia of a purely textual novel soon to become the hallmark of *Tel Quel*: resolutely "experimental" texts half-way between poetry and prose that did not represent anything but mimed or exhibited the very functioning of language. By showing the codes, cogs, and wheels of literary language, the production of a new poetic and political truth would, it was hoped, shatter the dominant repressive ideology.

In order to examine how the double helix, literary and ideological, which caught Theory in its vortex was set in motion, the volume put together by *Tel Quel* in the Fall of 1968 (the date has its importance in this period of swift changes), *Théorie d'ensemble*, proves crucial. The broad title aims at creating the impression of a group similar to the Surrealists, of a collective approach with a scientific slant, for it refers obliquely to the series of mathematical treatises on set theory (*théorie des ensembles*) written jointly by the anonymous group of Parisian mathematicians who called themselves Groupe Bourbaki. Since anonymity was not requested in this case as it would later be for Lacan's review *Scilicet*, it was replaced by a general agreement, a consensus as to who were the leaders in Theory. Hence, the volume highlights the key role of Foucault, Barthes, and Derrida, whose names are separated from all the other contributors and whose essays had appeared elsewhere. Foucault opens the volume with a reading of Robbe-Grillet whom he compares with Faye, Thibaudeau, Pleynet, and Sollers. Barthes continues with a piece on *Drame*, Sollers's novel of 1965. Derrida introduces the concept of *différance* and the unsigned introduction makes it clear that the group's "general theory" will resist being reduced either to formalism or structuralism. The key words that are proffered as so many new ruptures are *writing, text, the unconscious, history, work, trace, production, scene*.[65] Each of the three master theoreticians convoked has brought a new contribution – taken to be a "definitive" revelation – to the global problematic. Foucault is credited with the idea that texts are not representative but productive; Barthes demonstrates how writing scans history and decenters it; Derrida shows that writing can no longer be inscribed within the category of truth.[66] Based upon this significant convergence, a fourfold program posited the need "to unleash a movement . . . to elaborate concepts . . . to unfold a history/histories . . . to articulate a politics logically linked to a non-representational dynamics of writing."[67] The last point amounts to an admission that the political line of the review subscribes to the construction of dialectical materialism, a field in which other important masters are Lacan and Althusser. The program indicates the need to go back to a first "break" in history, not stopping at the avant-garde of the 1920s (Surrealism and Formalism relayed by structural linguistics), but rethinking the emblematic names of Lautréamont, Mallarmé, Marx, and Freud – whose main "discoveries," put together, roughly date from the second half of the nineteenth century.

If the writers' names change from year to year or from issue to issue, for some time this list of "precursors" (as Breton listed them in his manifestos) provides the basic formula upon which the review will endlessly revise and adapt. The systematic trope of *Tel Quel* is the linking of writers noted for their formal experiments or unorthodox and innovative writing (they may include Dante, Pound, Woolf, Céline, Joyce, Beckett, Bataille, Artaud) with the names of Marx and Freud for a time complemented by those of Lenin and Mao. Theory hesitates between a radical philosophical questioning of literary concepts and the more etymological sense of a "list" of authorities, or the ritual "procession" of tutelary figures invoked and yoked together. Patrick Ffrench's book on *Tel Quel* already opened with the double meaning contained in Theory, philosophical contemplation and collective witnessing, individual speculative thought and group procession of some chosen citizens.

> After speculation, theory returns to its processionary mode. This procession, or *traversée*, is not closed within the frame of a system, it is not a theory as structure, but a more sensuous, sinuous affair, a dance. *Tel Quel's* history exhibits this move from the terroristic closure of theory as speculation, a terror before the divine voice, to a dance across space, incarnating the divine voice in the body.[68]

If dance there was, it called up Parisian disco nights ushered in by Serge Gainbourg's playful reiterations and instrumentalizations, "Je t'aime – Moi non plus," as Theory's version of the song of lust united Marxism and Freudianism; the stomping binary beat of Marx and Freud was propelling Parisian intellectuals into a Saturday Night trance of Theory which was updating with a funkier sound the old Freudo–Marxism of the 1930s. For, more often than not, rhapsodic references to Althusser and Lacan functioned as shortcuts for what should read like "the real thought" of Marx and Freud. "Science" under these revolving strobe lights meant above all "Marx" after the epistemological break with Hegel's idealism and "Freud" without the biological naturalism of "instincts," fully endowed with Lacan's formula of "the Unconscious is structured like a language." The quotes around the names indicate that these are not the historical thinkers themselves but their author-functions that are envisioned, according to Foucault's revision of the concept of the "author" as an "inventor of discursivity."

The distribution of the contributors to *Théorie d'ensemble* reveals a subtle hierarchy: Sollers, Pleynet, and Baudry publish four pieces each while Houdebine, Kristeva, and Ricardou only two essays; Jean-Joseph Goux, Denis Roche, Pierre Rottenberg, Jacqueline Risset, and Jean Thibaudeau have only one contribution. The pieces still make for exciting reading today, if one can stand tics like the recurrent claim that all this is totally "scientific" or that the concept of "production" will solve all problems. Some of the best essays move from close readings to theories of literature, like those of Ricardou on Poe, Baudry on Freud, Pleynet on Sade or Eugene Sue, or start from their own production, as when we find Pleynet and Roche discussing Roche's scandalous and paradoxical anti-poetry and anti-poetics. A good debunking of some of the method-ological excesses evinced by certain texts came early enough, and the most balanced is probably to be found in an assessment pro-vided by Michael Riffaterre in 1969, when he showed how unten-able or far-fetched the formalism of some readings could be.

Riffaterre took the example of Ricardou's analysis of Poe's "Gold Bug" tale and pointed out how the word "huguenot" was misread as a sign of election, as the main character's ability to detect and decipher cryptograms. Riffaterre then demonstrated how this inter-pretation was based upon Baudelaire's translation and would not make sense in an American context in which "Protestant" is the norm and not the exception. More generally, he denounced the tendency among the *Tel Quelians* to take all the signifying elements as functioning equivalently, thus missing key differences between signifiers; for instance, in a typical case of over-interpretation, Ricardou believes that the signifier "gold" is hidden in the letters of "Golconda," a reason adduced for not using "Eldorado" (in spite of its recurring in a famous poem, as Riffaterre recalls).[69] Similarly, the name of Clairwill in Sade's *Story of Juliette* is glossed as "clear will" or "vile clarity" by Sollers and Ricardou respectively. Riffaterre has no difficulty in showing how arbitrary these assignations were, and needed a more commonsensical context. Yet one can distin-guish in Riffaterre's critical review an acknowledgment of mere methodological divergences, as when he reproaches Barthes for having made hasty generalizations about Tacitus's style which are nevertheless based upon observable stylistic features from real surprise at seeing the precise tools perfected by the Russian Formalists or Bahktin poorly used, exploited at random to justify fanciful associations.

The *Tel Quelians* would probably have answered impatiently, since what mattered for them at the time was not a more refined system of *explication de texte* but an unveiling of the workings of textuality – a revolutionary process, since it subverted the dominant ideologies ordering our current perception of the self, the world, and God, in a decentering which would then be used for cultural or political ends. The combination of Saussure, read by Derrida, of Marx, read by Althusser, and of Freud, read by Lacan, provided a fundamental trilogy mapping a new scientific and critical knowledge. This triptych would eventually lead Jean-Joseph Goux to a wholesale systematization of the theories of Lacan, Althusser, and Derrida: Goux established structural equivalences between money in capitalistic production and circulation, the phallus in psychoanalytic discourse, and the repression of writing in literary language. Such an ambitious but glib synthesis attracted the reproach of hasty assimilation, of structural homologies bled of any substance. The general theory seemed too obviously modeled after Marxist theories of economic circulation, the capitalistic money-fetishism turning into a caricature of the bourgeois specters hidden everywhere. All this, curiously, seemed to be elaborated in ignorance of the Frankfurt school and its critical theory. It would take another decade before the name of Benjamin would become significant again after the 1930s and his association with Bataille's group. However, the need to move beyond a rigid structuralist grid forced certain authors to look elsewhere for inspiration.

In this context, Kristeva used the mathematical logic inspired by the Tartu school of semiotics; she was conversant with Chomsky and Greimas, and freely quoted Peirce, Hegel, and Husserl. Roland Barthes was the first renowned critic who publicly acknowledged the fact that *Tel Quel* had brought about a major change, not only in the writing of literary theory, but in the very conception of literature, the two tending to blend together more and more.

One can witness how in the texts he publishes in the late 1960s, references to Kristeva (who had been his student) become more systematic and deferential. I have mentioned the new concepts such as intertextuality, the couple genotext/phenotext, the notion of signifying practice, of "signifiance" opposed to "signification," the idea of an infinite productivity identified with a "text" that is strongly delineated from the "work," which mark for Barthes a shift from purely "scientific" and potentially boring engagements with semiotics – let us not forget how Barthes described boredom as his peculiar form of hysteria in the photographic album of his own *Roland Barthes* – to a new set of issues in which dynamism, productivity, and infinity are constantly invoked. Barthes's wonderful *S/Z* (also published in the *Tel Quel* series in 1970) manages to let the two semiotic systems function side by side. Other critics protested at the same time, less in the name of traditional values than of scientific rigor. Thus, in a scathing attack, Jacques Roubaud and Philippe Lusson use their first-hand knowledge of mathematics and logic to demonstrate that almost all the logical or mathematical formulas used by Kristeva in her first book are redundant or contradictory: they either underline decoratively what has been relatively well expressed in plain language, or mix up incompatible systems of formalization[70] – this some thirty years before Sokal and Bricmont.

The attack corresponded with a troubled period linked with splits and struggles that marked the end of the 1960s: the break-up between Sollers and Jean-Pierre Faye; the only intellectual and writer whose stature was equal to his led Faye to launch the rival magazine *Change* – also published by Le Seuil – whose very name intends to contradict the alleged statism of *Tel Quel*. On the other hand, a review like *Poétique* founded by three eminent former collaborators, Genette, Todorov, and Cixous, aimed less at cultural critique than at prolonging a serious and more academic investigation of the practical consequences of the theory of literature. This, coupled with an often paradoxical politicization of the review – *Tel Quel* members became close allies of the French Communist Party just before May 1968 – which led most of them to keep their distance from a youthful movement considered to be too Dadaist and playful, while the same insistence on radical breaks and dogmatic righteousness led them to become Maoist in 1971, just when some unpleasant truths about the Cultural Revolution begin to emerge. Consequently, pre- and post-1968 Surrealism is denounced as idealist and Hegelian, along with Blanchot, as we have seen. More curiously even, when the review lost its appeal for a majority of intellectuals upset by its modishness (the good British critic in charge of *Screen*, Stephen Heath, broke with them violently), it increased its publication run, special issues reaching more than 20,000 copies (whereas the usual run would be between 3,000 and 5,000 before). The fascination for China led Sollers, Kristeva, and their friends to some efforts at documentation, but their fatal blunder was to take a group-trip to China in the spring of 1974 (Sollers and Kristeva went with Pleynet, Barthes, and Wahl), thus confronting their dreams with a reality that resisted ideological showcasing. Kristeva brought back a beautiful if deluded essay about *Chinese Women*. However, disillusionment and dissatisfaction with a non–Western utopia soon crept in, especially for Barthes, and the Chinese fountainhead of youth ran dry. In 1976 Houdebine denounced the dead-end of language in Marxism, while Sollers discovered that Maoism was an updated Stalinism, a point that had not escaped earlier observers of the Cultural Revolution. In spite of a shriller insistence on the necessary link between politics and literature, the review would often evince great political naïveté, all the while showing amazing skills at tactics of literary self-promotion.

The year 1976 brought about a last reversal in alliances when the review opened its pages to the "new philosophers" who had launched a wholesale attack not just on Stalinism but on Marx, up to then sacrosanct. Suddenly Marx was blamed for all the totalitarian monsters generated in his name. Alexandr Solzhenitsyn and Joseph Brodsky became the heroes of André Glucksmann, Bernard-Henri Lévy, and Maria-Antonietta Macciocchi. Resistance to communism was now fashionable. Predictably, Sollers allowed himself to be seduced by the new philosophers' rediscovery of religion, either as the Jewish foundation embraced by Levy or as a more baroque Catholicism that might have been there all the time in Lacan's background. And the former enemy constituted by capitalist America was seen in a new light as the place of a new bodily fusion of dance, music, and freedom in a special issue devoted to the USA in 1977. Thus, by 1980, it became clear that the review had lost its focus and its impetus. Its impact on French culture was diminishing. Going along with Barthes's canonization in high schools, *Tel Quel*'s concepts had been on the whole accepted. Its main ideas had been fully underwritten by the cutting-edge fringe of scholars and professors. On the other hand, the denunciation of totalitarian ideologies had more clout when it came from right-wing magazines. Sollers appeared as the puppet-master of a moribund avant-garde that had lost its master-signifiers one after the other, and when he quarreled with François Wahl, the editor of Le Seuil, who had objected to the publication of *Women* (1983) because of its transparent satire of the milieu they had frequented, with vitriolic portraits of Cixous, Lacan, Althusser, Barthes, Derrida, and famous feminist theoreticians, the review needed to be reinvented. Sollers and Pleynet chose Gallimard to launch *L'Infini*. A page had been turned, and Le Seuil editors, who had intelligently speculated on the rise of "human sciences" and multiplied rival reviews, could then conclude with a general disaffection with High Theory. Besides, all of a sudden Sartre, Barthes, and Lacan had died within a year, soon followed by Althusser and Foucault.

One should not grudge one's admiration: in retrospect, the work accomplished by *Tel Quel* has been enormous if muddleheaded, and the particular exhilaration discernible among French participants to the Baltimore conference in 1966 no doubt owes something to the atmosphere *Tel Quel* helped to create. It has been evoked by Sollers in *Women* with some self-congratulation when "S." reminisces on the crucial cultural function played by his "little avant-garde revue," a review "Which is now, thanks to S.'s grim perseverance, a kind of international institution . . . It has published the best work of Werth, Lutz, Fals, and many others . . . Established their reputation."[71] The transparent pseudonyms allude to Barthes, Althusser, and Lacan: even if one notes some exaggeration, this describes well how any avant-garde will, if it is successful, turn into an "institution." *Tel Quel* transformed literary theory, gave it its edge and wide impact, while allowing a few literary and critical landmarks to be published: the discovery of the Formalists and of Bakhtin in France is due to them, as is the wide appeal of the theses developed by Barthes and Derrida. On the literary front, Maurice Roche's

Compact remained the group's most prized avant-garde text. Printed in 1966, it was later rediscovered by a younger and different avant-garde. Just before its demise, *Tel Quel* also helped Guyotat publish his scandalously subversive novels on the Algerian war.

My general claim is that, despite its obvious shortcomings, much of what we call Theory today finds a concrete realization in *Tel Quel's* syncretic energies, an unstable amalgam that lasted only a few years; for a moment, the time of a lyrical illusion, it looked as if one could marshal together the concepts of Foucault, Althusser, Bataille, Derrida, Barthes, Lacan, and Kristeva. Literature was spoken of as a signifying practice whose subversive power interacted with the social context that produced it. Interdisciplinary approaches to poetry, painting, dance, and philosophy would trigger productive synergies. Avant-garde strategies deduced from close readings of Sade, Artaud, Roussel, Lautréamont, or Joyce were applied to more conventional writers like Dante, Donne, or Hugo. Finally, Theory appeared as less assured than it claimed, since it was constantly hesitating between terrorism and theology, its recurrent hysteria significantly caught up between verbal dogmatism and endless dissidence.

The main shortcomings of *Tel Quel* derive from the discrepancy between the theoretical program and the literature it produced. I have mentioned Maurice Roche, Denis Roche and Guyotat, but they were relatively peripheral figures in the "group." There was never for *Tel Quel* the possibility of adducing unmistakable masterpieces as proof of the soundness of the theory, as was the case with English-language modernism, which could boast of having generated *Tarr*, *Ulysses*, *The Waste land*, and *Mrs. Dalloway* almost at the same time. The irony latent in Sollers's reputation comes from the fact that *Women*, his best-known novel, is, after all, rather straightforward as to plot and not very innovative in style, like all those written by Sollers afterwards. If he achieved what he wanted— to keep in touch with a large audience – no Theory was needed to justify the simple pleasure a writer can take in his own skills. The same cannot be said of Julia Kristeva's novels *Les Samouraïs* (1990) and *Le Vieil homme et les loups* (1991) which were terrible flops. Once or twice, Theory was called to the rescue; thus Kristeva used skillfully her own theory of the semiotic as opposed to the symbolic in an effort to defend the curiously stilted dialogues, the conventional descriptions, and the hackneyed prose. She describes how she would prepare her writing by diving deep down into her past and her unconscious:

> To this, then, rhythms, melodies, scansions are added – as so many pre-syntactic or "semiotic" approaches to what language has become for me: a varied music, then, connects French and Slavic vocalizations in me, generating a strange sound, a sound that some people find in bad taste, pathetic and finally not very French. At any rate, this creates a monstrous sound and a monstrous intimacy, more monstrous perhaps than that of the giants at the end of *Time Regained*.[72]

No Theory can save, alas, from such a risky proximity with monumental "giants." At least Barthes had systematized the application of the Lacanian term of *jouissance* to these avant-garde texts he found so tantalizingly opaque and experimental in their attempt to disclose the pure functioning of textuality which made them boring, therefore "interesting." To be honest, most of the texts written by Sollers and his acolytes at the height of the Theory years are unreadable today. The critical readings remain while the impact of the literary avant-garde in terms of style and language is quasi-nonexistent. Was that too high a price to pay for Theory to reign?

3

Theory, Science, Technology

When Barthes was promoting his hard version of structuralism, disseminating views he would soon repudiate, an endeavor for which he was taken to task by Paul de Man as we have seen in the Baltimore debate, he presented literary history as scholarship dominated by concepts that tended to allegorize periods and trends. For instance, the modern period, ushered in by Flaubert and Mallarmé, would mark the end of a "classical" writing loaded with all the sins of bourgeois possessiveness, dull common sense, and a naive belief in language's transparency; after this "revolution," literature would turn into a problematic of language and begin its endless revolution in the name of writing. We have seen how the "writing degree zero" exemplified by Camus or the practitioners of the *nouveau roman* would lead to pure literature, or Blanchot's ideal of the "neuter," a neutral or blank voice deprived of all traditional markers heralding literary style. Thus literature would be set free as sheer literarity, discharged from usual communicative functions and embarking on the exploration of particular uses of language. Barthes was nevertheless aware of the dangerously mythical position he was made to occupy, as he tried to argue in reply to de Man. If everything that he produces as a critic merely perpetuated a mythology of literary language which took writing as the main signifier of literary myth,[1] could the science of structural linguistics that had so far helped Lévi-Strauss structure his analysis of myth and society also provide a validly universalizing principle? The arbitrary nature of the linguistic sign had received a foundational role in this critical reading of mythological systems, and we know that Barthes was easily "sickened" by the false naturalization of a language condoning all sorts of ideological exploitations: "This nausea is like the one I feel before the arts which refuse to choose between *physis* and *antiphysis*, using the first as an ideal and the second as an economy. Ethically, it is quite low to wish to play on these two levels at once."[2] The enemy to destroy by all means resided in the stronghold of a Nature all the more wicked as it was inhabited by ghostly signs. In this battle, a scientific outlook would never preclude an ethical position.

This fundamental tenet gave Barthes a strategic standpoint from which he engaged in a systematic criticism of the illusions pertaining to the naturalization of form. Literature would play a crucial role in this process since the transformation of life into text often implies taking form for content, reducing history to nature, allowing textual production to revert to ideological consumption. It seems that Barthes would agree with Adorno in the debate I have sketched earlier, since both point to the need for denouncing the mechanism by which a denial of History reconstitutes the treacherous world of myth. Barthes, however, is also close to Benjamin insofar as his readings of contemporary myths keep a Brechtian edge: as in Brecht's theater, the critical outlook creates a distance from which the audience will judge and understand instead of passively identifying with people or events. Yet, for a time, Barthes seemed to believe in the possibility of a science which would be valid for all narratives, and he displayed his skill at synthesis in his theory of a "Structural Analysis of Narratives" that managed to combine the approaches of Greimas, Brémond, Propp, Jakobson, and other Russian Formalists by distinguishing between functions such as "request," "aid," and "punishment" in the logic of the plot, then actions (characters are "actants" in a literary praxis that questions the status of subjectivity), and finally the level of narration or discourse, implying a narrator and addressees. While Barthes first held that semiology was a part of linguistics considered as the main scientific paradigm, he later abandoned that position and investigated all possible ways in which scientific approaches would be pluralized, reaching beyond the text, myth, or fashion system to the activity that produces it as a discourse.

The Science of the Impossible

This prodigal energy underpins *S/Z*, an excessively exhaustive analysis of Balzac's story "Sarrasine," in a virtuoso theoretical *potlatch* exploiting and exploding all the rhetorical resources of a "classical" text in order to demonstrate that the story's layering of codes undoes any opposition between classicism and modernity. The book stresses plurality and combines all possible semiological strategies, and by flirting consciously with all the modes of over-interpretation ends up reading like a musical score, and becomes almost a work of art. Textuality is literalized as a weaving of codes, a braiding of textures, while a fine-sliced textualization is seen as a hermeneutic progression through codes, an odyssey in which writers and readers move on an equal basis. Textuality is constituted by the interplay of codes whose symbolic enmeshment rules out any origin, including, of course, the ownership of the text's meaning in the name of authority. The reflexive momentum of the critical process leads to the ineluctable awareness that science functions as another myth, and to a questioning of the myth of science still upheld by fellow *Tel Quelians*. For a while, Barthes thought that the question of science could be replaced with the issue of plea-sure. Rather than ask "What do we know about texts?" it seemed more legitimate to wonder: "How do we enjoy texts?" A distinc-) enjoy tion elaborated in *S/Z* comes in handy and opposes "writerly" to "readerly" texts, that is texts that merely obey logics of passive con-sumption and texts that stimulate the reader's active participation. This generates an alternative of either textual *plaisir* or textual *jouis-sance*. *Jouissance* calls up a violent, climactic bliss closer to loss, death, fragmentation, and the disruptive rapture experienced when trans-gressing limits, whereas *plaisir* simply hints at an easygoing enjoy-ment, more stable in its reenactment of cultural codes. This freewheeling use of Lacan's terminology aims not so much at dis-crediting pleasure in favor of sublimated types of enjoyment as at creating a language capable of concretely describing the effect of words on bodies and, conversely, of bodies on words. The modern text *de jouissance* may often be boring, tedious, and repetitive, yet it concentrates energy and strikes the innermost core of the reading-writing subject.

Barthes started bridging the gap he himself had posited in more and more overtly autobiographical books, like *Roland Barthes by Roland Barthes* in 1975. He was irresistibly driven to a piece of writing that would do justice to all his changing positions while drawing an ideogram of his many selves. This book must be read "as if spoken by a character in a novel," which introduced Barthes's writerly moment, the phase of his so-called "moralities". Barthes came very close to being a novelist in his own right, and enacted modernist paradigms with a vengeance since his mode of success was to be a failure, as Sartre said of Baudelaire and Flaubert, as Blanchot said of Mallarmé, and as Beckett repeatedly said of himself. Thus Barthes's "fiction," programmed to have been autobiographically Proustian, remained potential, tentative, elusive, in fact yet to be written unless we take *A Lover's Discourse* as his unique "play for voices" like, say, *Under Milk Wood* with its dramatic method of presentation blending quotations, personal remarks, and subtle generalizations, and *Camera Lucida* as a last personal elegy for his mother. This moving disclosure of a son's love facing an absent photograph through which he could mourn his mother was disguised as a study of photography that shockingly recanted all previous semiological approaches. Whereas in many former essays Barthes had stressed the artificial nature of such a medium and its ideological power, he now identifies photography as pure reference; it immediately bespeaks a past presence, and its ultimate signifier is the death and absence of the loved one. Barthes took apart the powerful machine he had built, to the dismay of his followers or commentators like Jonathan Culler. At least this gesture confirms a pattern that has been observed in all major theoreticians: they are caught up in a contradiction that forces them to invent systems that borrow from various sciences or tend to the condition of science (Derrida has toyed for some time with the idea of a "grammatology," the mirage of a positive "science of writing") while denying if not the scientificity of the system at least the mechanical or automatic applications of the methods to texts.

Barthes's own recapitulation of his career should not be taken as an endless aporia of auto-critique, an infinite regress in the hope of postulating an elsewhere of theory that would still be theoretical. As we saw Foucault perform it in *Archeology of Knowledge*, there is here an attempt at transcending all previous positions and discourses so as to move with the mobile subjectivity constituted as a hole or gap:

> Let us follow this trajectory again. At the work's source, the opacity of social relations, a false Nature; the first impulse, the first shock then, is to demystify (*Mythologies*); then when the demystification is immobilized in repetition, it must be displaced: semiological *science* (then postulated) tries to stir, to vivify, to arm the mythological gesture or pose by endowing it with a method; this science is encumbered in its turn with a whole imaginary: the goal of a semiological science is replaced by the (often very grim) science of the semiologists; hence, one must sever oneself from that, one must introduce into this rational imaginary the texture of desire, the claims of the body; this, then, is the Text, the Theory of the Text. But again the Text risks paralysis: it repeats itself, counterfeits itself in lusterless texts, testimonies to a demand for readers, not for a desire to please: the Text tends to degenerate into prattle. Where to go next? That is where I am now.[3]

As is clear from this passage, science is not repudiated because it is wrong, but because it is boring. Why not then extol science precisely in the name of a boredom that comes so close to bliss? As *The Pleasure of the Text* puts it so well: "Boredom is not far from bliss [*jouissance*]: it is bliss seen from the shores of pleasure."[4] Should one distinguish between a good and a bad boredom then? What is still condoned in the name of avant-garde asceticism or political commitment cannot hold here because of a theoretical excess that finally threatens textuality. I believe that it would be very short-sighted to blame Barthes's progressive disenchantment with Theory on a personal *acedia*, a hedonistic quest grown stale or petering out in tricks and belletristics. The passage I have quoted earlier says very explicitly that the "Theory of the Text" ended up killing texts, generating repetitious therefore uninteresting (or rather, merely "interesting") writing, be it the writing of so-called "criticism" or of experimental texts – the two being of course almost impossible to differentiate at the time of *Tel Quel*.

Here we approach one of the major pitfalls of Theory, namely the ease with which it produces standard interpretations, repetitive or dull writing. Barthes was one of the first to react with uncharacteristic vehemence or flamboyance to this danger, whereas most theoreticians felt the need to either move elsewhere or break with the protocols implied by their "methods." A similar note has been more recently sounded by Derrida when he summed up the process leading to the transformation of his deconstructive problematic into a methodology that would be applicable everywhere; in a quasi-parody of Descartes's *Discourse on Method* he describes the introduction into American universities, especially in literature departments, of paradigms he had launched and how these soon generated a network of "possibilities and powers" immediately imported and implemented:

> That is to say, organized bodies of rules, of procedures and techniques, in a word, *methods*, know-how applicable in a recurrent fashion. One could even formulate or formalize (and I applied myself in this way at first) a certain consistency in these laws which made possible reading processes at once critical and critical of the idea of critique, processes of close reading, which could reassure those who in or outside the wake of new criticism or some other formalism felt it necessary to legitimize this ethics of close reading or internal reading. And among the examples of these procedural or formalizing formulae that I had proposed . . . there was the reversal of a hierarchy. After having reversed a binary opposition, whatever it may be – speech/writing, man/woman, spirit/matter, signifier/signified, signified/signifier, master/slave, and so on – and having liberated the subjugated and submissive term, one then proceeded to the generalization of this latter in new traits, producing a different concept, for example another concept of writing such as trace, *différance*, gramme, text, and so on.[5]

It is rare to see the "inventor" of a critical method present such an honest assessment of what has been, it is true, too often systematized into simple conceptual tricks under the guise of deconstruction. Not that he engages in debunking pastiche or contorted self-parody; the assessment of what has passed as deconstruction nevertheless attests to the validity of the problematics – what is unbearable is that it turns into an easy refrain, and can "function" almost regardless of the text taken as example or simple pretext.

We are caught in a delicate dilemma: the more powerful a theory is, the more possibilities it will open in the name of concepts (like, say, "difference" or "the subaltern") which then are streamlined and mass-produced. No theory can establish itself without such conceptual tools or without at least promising "handles" which in their turn provide new "purchases" on texts or cultural artifacts. But the novelty soon fades, and another gadget has to be invented: Derrida has often provided long lists of the terms he would devise one after the other, "*différance*," "trace," "hymen," "*parergon*," "aporia," "undecidability" among them. Their "theory," that is their procession as a series of idiomatic and untranslatable signifiers, or better, "signatures," would ideally aim at preventing the instrumental closure of Theory. The awareness that this movement could not continue indefinitely led Derrida to take stock of the concept of instrumentality quite candidly:

> This slightly instrumentalizing implementation tended to reduce the impetus of the languages, the desire, the arrival so to speak, the future, of deconstructions, and might well arrest them at the possible: that is, a body of possibilities, of faculties, indeed of facilities, in a word, a body of easily reproducible means, methods, and technical procedures, hence useful, utilizable; a body of rules and knowledge; a body of theoretical, methodological, epistemological knowledge; a body of powerful know-how that would be at once understandable and offered for didactic transmission, susceptible of acquiring the academic status and dignity of a quasi-interdisciplinary discipline.[6]

Derrida will typically opt for the "impossible," and after a survey of all the paradoxes, aporias, and double-binds his thinking has traversed, he requests precisely the contrary of such an instrumental reduction: his concepts keep only their relevance if they open to the event as event, that is precisely to an event that will exceed any program, a radical novelty incommensurable with protocols elaborated after having computed logical possibilities from which one will finally be chosen. On the contrary, by reiterating the old slogan dating from May 1968: "Demand the impossible!," deconstruction finds a way back to what I have called the hystericization of Theory. It asserts the sentence that Lacan claimed he heard in couples whose mutual desire was fading: "I ask you to refuse what I give you because it is not the real thing." Like the erratic desire of the hysteric, a desire that can never be satisfied because it refuses any satisfaction in advance, deconstruction is poised on a threshold between the amassed weight of death (dead texts, dead signs, dead writers) that together makes up a whole tradition and a messianism which promises "new life," or life as new, in the future. The future of Theory would lie there, in the endless deferral of a Figaro's promise: "Tomorrow, I will shave you for free." For Theory, tomorrow *has* to be another day.

Such a discourse risks being all too baffling for students who crave clear certainties and love nothing like protocols, cool tools, handy handles or even better, "power tools."[7] How can we tell them something like: "Do whatever you please, just avoid boring me!" when they want to go home with a power drill preferably accompanied by its instruction manual? Boredom is indeed the reaction triggered by imitative discourses, and boredom was massively institutionalized in American universities when Theory gave birth to endless copy-cat readings killing any sense of the "new" in texts; quite often, this hardnosed insistence on fundamental issues like Platonism or metaphysics was totally blind to the singularity of a text, to its unique eventness. It is obviously vital that Theory avoid its reduction to mere methods or protocols of reading, for otherwise it will only find in a text the concepts it brings to it. I still recall my dismay in the early 1990s at finding my US graduate students giving me unstintingly what they thought I was requesting, namely endless regurgitations of Derrida, Lacan, or Cixous, in frustratingly competent but unenlightened mimetic readings.

Derrida found himself confronted by this predicament when his disciple and friend Geoffrey Bennington had the task of preparing a guide to his works. He was at his most Barthesian in the cunning strategy he deployed in the *Jacques Derrida* authored by Geoffrey Bennington and himself. This time, Derrida had not been writing the analysis of his own corpus but was asked to comment on a critical synthesis while preserving its openness. An introductory note announces the rules of the game:

> G.B. would have liked to systematize J.D.'s thought to the point of turning it into an interactive program, which, in spite of its difficulty, would in principle be accessible to any user. As what is at stake in J.D.'s work is to show how any such system must remain essentially open, this undertaking was doomed to failure from the start . . . In order to demonstrate the ineluctable necessity of the failure, our contract stipulated that J.D., having read G.B.'s text, would write something escaping the proposed systematization, surprising it.[8]

As the note adds, Derrida's "response" did surprise Bennington, who was not allowed to revise then what he had written. What one discovers in a series of running footnotes – 59 to be precise, as Derrida was 59 when he wrote them – is a stunningly provocative text entitled "Circumfession" and whose main themes, endlessly spliced and intertwined, are circumcision and confession, especially in Saint Augustine's version of the genre. Unabashedly autobiographical, this vibrant "confession" extends the limits of the philosophical essay: one will be privy to many poignant details about the philosopher's mother and grandmother, his own circumcision and private obsessions connected to it. The effort to push Theory elsewhere, to a private "beyond" dialoguing with a doctrinal corpus that the theoretician cannot totally disown is altogether spectacular, while demonstrating untapped resources in deconstructive strategies.

Can Literary Criticism Teach Virtue?

Could this gesture be repeated? Could anyone do this? Obviously not. The question insists: if the method teaches that it is not

repeatable, that its concepts have to undo themselves as they decon-
struct other texts or other concepts, what then can be taught? Can
one just say to students: "Surprise me!" as one would say: "Please
make me laugh"? If it all boils down to saying: "Just be clever and
sensitive, the rest will follow," what is the point of teaching the
theory of literature and Theory – if, anyhow, one is sent back to
one's private subjectivity in the end? Can excellence, can the highest
competence in literary criticism, be taught? This is exactly the question debated by Plato in *Protagoras*, a dialogue through which I have
to make a brief detour. The main issue in the dialogue is the following: can one teach virtue? Protagoras, perhaps the most famous
"Sophist" – let us not forget that universities as we know them
today owe a lot, if not everything, to the pedagogical efforts of the
Sophists in fifth-century Athens – and who is often remembered
mainly for his famous "Man is the measure of all things," will of
course argue that virtue can be taught; otherwise, how could he
ask handsome sums of money from his students who all hope to
further their careers with the techniques they have learned? Conversely, Socrates will deny that virtue can be taught: right opinion
inheres in everyone, what matters is the dialectical movement that
can turn one's soul toward the contemplation of the good. Inneism
seems to be opposed to culturalism, in the same way as sophistic relativism bordering on skepticism (Protagoras also held that
"nothing could be proved but everything refuted") clashes with
Plato's essentialism or foundationalism.

As soon as the debate progresses, however, things get more
complex. If Socrates appears as Plato's mouthpiece in his search for
an absolute value that will be used to discredit sophistic pedagogy,
when it comes to practical examples Plato tends to reduce value to
knowledge, while Protagoras seems to believe in values that are not
derived from knowledge. This is nowhere more visible than in the
long and at times hilarious discussion over a well-known (at the
time) poem by Simonides. The choice of a literary discussion is an
important moment in the strategy of a Sophist like Protagoras, since
he believed like all Sophists that the art of textual interpretation was
a key factor in any pedagogy. Socrates and Protagoras have had a
hard time agreeing on even the simplest procedures pertaining to
their dialogue. Protagoras, more skilled in traditional eloquence and

mythical parallels, prefers giving long speeches to which other speeches will respond; Socrates insists on a purely dialogical method progressing through short questions and answers. With the help of Alcibiades, he has forced Protagoras (who has first given an impassioned and convincing speech on Prometheus, the demi-god who gave technology to men and who is for him the founder of civilization) to agree to pursuing a maieutic dialogue. Protagoras begins this second round with a statement to the effect that he believes in literary competence as a mark of good education ("I consider, Socrates, that a most important part of a man's education is being knowledgeable about poetry"),[9] which stresses an idea most of us would agree on, I suppose, that literary criticism helps develop critical faculties allied with a concern for a precise and rigorous use of language. He immediately challenges Socrates by taking a precise example. He quotes a famous lyrical poem by Simonides in which he has detected a contradiction: as the poem assesses what constitutes excellence, it is crucial for the Sophist to identify Socrates's view on two antagonistic versions: on the one hand Simonides begins by saying that "It is hard . . . to become a truly good man," but in a later stanza he takes issue with Pittacus who had erred, according to the poet, when he said that "it is hard to be noble."

Socrates, who has imprudently confessed that he knows the poem quite well (he has "studied it closely") and subscribes to its meaning, is taken aback by the demonstration of the inconsistency: how could he fail to see that the famous poet contradicted himself hopelessly? Socrates then takes a blow like a half-stunned boxer: "my eyes went dim and I felt giddy, as if I had been hit by a good boxer" (339 e). To gain time, he desperately tries to find help from one of the bystanders, Prodicus, a teacher of rhetoric whose specialty was establishing nuanced distinctions between near-synonyms. Of course, the philologist will willingly oblige and confirm that "to be noble" has nothing to with "becoming noble." This semantic sleight of hand will not carry Socrates very far, for Protagoras hits him even harder: "Your defence, Socrates, involves a worse mistake than the one you are defending him against . . . It would show great stupidity on the poet's part if he says that it is so easy to keep excellence once you have it, when that's the most difficult thing of all, as everyone agrees" (339 d–340 e). Socrates again resorts to

Prodicus's linguistic expertise based on knowledge of different dialects, and attempts to equate "hard" with "bad" (Pittacus would be reproached for saying "it is bad to be noble"!). However, this does not sway Protagoras in the least, and Socrates has to abandon this effort as a red herring and a "joke." By a curious return to the mythical and digressive method, it is now Socrates who delivers a long speech of almost six pages, on the meaning of the poem, a speech full of indirection and irony, almost farcical at times. In a vein of infectious parody, Socrates supposes that Pittacus admired the excellence of Spartan education, a military and xenophobic training that wished to limit one's utterance to pithy sayings like "It is hard to be good." To which Simonides would reply: "No, but rather to *become* a good man, Pittacus, is hard in truth" (343 d). While he introduces an entire Bakhtinian dialogism with open-ended and double-voiced sentences, Socrates twists words and meanings more than once, reaching at one point a reversal from the opposition originally laid down by Protagoras; thus he has Simonides intone at one point: "But you, Pittacus, say that it is hard to be noble; but in fact to become noble is hard, but possible, but to be noble is impossible" (344 e). Taking examples from writing and medical science, Socrates concludes his defense of Simonides's poem and therefore his attack on Pittacus in these terms: "it is impossible to be a good man, good all the time, that is, but it is possible to become good and for the same man to become bad. And the best, who are good for longest, are those whom the gods love" (345 c).

I will just pause here to let the dialectical couple of the possible and the impossible reverberate for a while, echoing as it were with what we heard Derrida pleading for: a method that criticizes all methods by reaching an impossibility, an aporia from which another angle or viewpoint should be generated. It is clear that behind Socrates's back, Plato is arguing for the impossibility of a science of literary criticism. When he shows us Socrates outdoing Protagoras in ruses, semantic quibbles, and dialogical subterfuges, he aims at discrediting criticism as a valid *techne*. By showing us how Socrates can discourse endlessly on a few words, he means that it is not too difficult to perform tricks like those of Protagoras. The main conclusion he wishes to reach, and for which he receives the full assent of all the audience, is that it is not worth continuing the exegetical exercise ("let's leave the question of lyric and other kinds of poetry," 347 b–c). Moreover, in his hyper-sophistic mode of reasoning, Socrates does not hesitate to twist the meaning of Simonides's poem by making him endorse the kind of rationalist morality he upholds in the rest of the dialogue:

> For Simonides was not so uneducated as to say he praised those who do nothing bad of their own free will, as if there were some people who do bad things freely. For I am pretty much of this opinion, that no intelligent man believes that anyone does wrong freely or acts shamefully and badly of his own free will. (345 e)

Why was it important for Protagoras to seize on a contradiction in a famous poem? Protagoras uses the literary analysis as a continuation of his mythical evocation of *techne* by other means: after myths of gods and heroes, we engage with famous poets whose verses are known by heart. By exposing how contradictory poetic statements about virtue or excellence are, he does not remain at a formalist standpoint,[10] but hopes to prove how contradictory we are when we talk about virtue or excellence. It would be idle to reproach him for not having exposed his own views on virtue, first because Socrates does not allow him to do so at the occasion of the poem, secondly because this is the aim of the whole dialogue.

However, in his own interpretation of the poem, Socrates has swallowed Simonides: the dialogism he has invested the poem with has finally been absorbed by his own criteria, among which intelligence figures primarily. For instance, if Simonides occasionally praised tyrants or evil persons in his poems, this was not done of his free will, he was coerced by circumstances; this is what Simonides sees in Pittacus according to Socrates, who then quotes a line which resounds ironically in the context: "For the generation of fools is endless" (346 c). Thus the main thesis of the dialogue has been asserted: virtue is knowledge and vice is ignorance; nobody will do evil willingly or knowingly; one cannot teach virtue as one can teach how to memorize a poem, but virtue consists in understanding the abstract rules that govern technique. Conversely, Protagoras's position seems closer to that of an American New Critic, always intent upon detecting ambiguities, tensions, and paradoxes in poems. He would point to these less with the view of proving that poetic language is brimming over with mutually incompatible perspectives, hence its richness, but in the hope of confounding all foundationalist pretensions at certainty. However, what "conclusion" can we reach if we see that the dialogue between the two philosophers foregrounds its very paradoxes and contradictions? At the end of a long and inconclusive discussion on courage and knowledge, Socrates himself stresses the "absurdity" of the situation by letting the (in) "conclusion" they have reached – one might say the contested tangle of meaning traversed by the dialogue we have just heard or read – say to them, in a remarkable prosopopoeia:

> You, Socrates, began by saying that excellence can't be taught, and now you are insisting on the opposite, trying to show that all things are knowledge, justice, soundness of mind, even courage, from which it would follow that excellence most certainly could be taught . . . Protagoras, on the other hand, first assumed that it can be taught, but now seems to be taking the opposite view and insisting that it turns out to be practically anything rather than knowledge; and so it most certainly couldn't be taught. (361 a–c)

Again, Plato's strategy is more cunning than it seems: what matters in this neat chiastic reversal offering too easily a null result is above all to let Protagoras renounce his own thesis. We need to recall that he had started with two apparently irrefutable arguments: when the Athenians have to take political decisions that entail specific knowledge, they ask experts to provide scientific data, yet when they have to debate issues of justice, they assume that every citizen should decide according to the lights of his conscience (322 c–323 a). Besides, excellent men often find that their sons fail to follow in their steps on the path of virtue, which tends to prove that virtue is a matter of education. But if Socrates demonstrates the reverse, namely that all these virtues simply consist in mobilizing the right kind of knowledge at the right moment, the apparent contradiction is not really damning: Socrates is in a good position now to show that it is not "man" who is the measure of all things but a knowledge that will look to mathematics as paradigm. Excellence can then be taught in the sense that one would be either silly or perverse to refuse to take an "objective" measure by which all actions, passions, and qualities are determined. The real enemy was not the literary seductions deployed by rhetoricians for hire but purely and simply anthropocentric relativism.

Protagoras does not really contradict himself either, if one assumes that knowledge can be relativistic, that is if one can teach broad principles, a logical, literary, and rhetorical know-how leading to personal excellence in such a way that these self-help techniques will not always work or produce standard results; of course, if this is denied, then his thesis falls to the ground. This is why the debate on poetry assumes such an important role, and why Nietzsche was so right when he had stressed that, if Socrates had forced Plato to renounce playwriting, to burn all his youthful productions in the manner of Sophocles or Euripides, he had never really abandoned the dramatic genre in his philosophical dialogues. All the dialogic resources of drama are mobilized against an intellectual game (in the discussion, a game clearly dominated by Socrates) that consists in discussing a text "as such," that is in the absence of its author. Even if Protagoras is not exactly a "New Critic" as we have seen, Plato demonstrates the futility of New Criticism when he criticizes the idea that a text is a text and nothing else. He does this by destroying the idea that its formal or rhetorical properties can be teased out by close reading. Plato is in that respect much closer to Theory than it seems, since one of the crucial differences between New Criticism and Theory has consisted in the critique of the notion of "leaving the text alone," cut off from its context, to be sure defined more as a library than the world out there. For even when Derrida said that there was "no outside the text" in a statement that has triggered countless controversies, he did not insist on textual autonomy, as has often been thought, but on the aporetic impossibility of deciding exactly where "text" would end and "world" would begin.

Thus we see a sulking Protagoras ruing a lost opportunity for brilliant literary criticism (what is more, he is chided by Alcibiades, Socrates's young and handsome lover – a lover Socrates had spurned

107

at the beginning so as to be able to converse freely with the great Protagoras – for being unduly silent and churlish). Socrates attempts to nail the coffin of Greek lit. crit. even before it was born; to this aim, he conjures up an image of degradation that casts literary theory in a totally unfavorable light. "For the discussion of poetry strikes me as very like a drinking-party of common, vulgar fellows; for people of that sort, who for lack of education can't entertain one another over the wine with their own conversation, put up the price of flute-girls, and pay large sums to hear the sound of flute instead of their own talk" (347 c–d). Well-educated people will on the contrary renounce the seduction of facile entertainment (as is done by common agreement at the beginning of the *Symposium*) and will hence engage with each other through responsible discourse. By showing the spineless irresponsibility of literary criticism, Plato has in fact demonstrated the unaccountability of literature in general. The new generation of philosophers he calls for will have no need of poetry or poets, since "you can't question them about what they say, but in most cases when people quote them, one says the poet means one thing and one another, and they argue over points which can't be established with any certainty" (347 e). In spite of some affinities, we have finally butted into the prejudice that Derrida had so early and so pertinently denounced as Plato's recurrent prevention against writing in the name of a living speech which can keep memory alive and live up to its ethical responsibility, i.e. logocentrism; if Derrida had made the demonstration a propos the *Phaedrus* in "Plato's Pharmacy,"[11] and has returned to Plato a few times since, the deep suspicion of literary writing remains a constant in Plato's doctrine.

At least, in this impassioned peroration, Plato has made his point clear after Socrates's debunking of literary sophistics, as if we had reached a *Quod erat demonstrandum*. A text will never allow you to get to the core or essence of any issue, and we too, like gentlemen of good breeding should "leave the poets aside and conduct our argument independently, testing the truth of the matter and our own capacities" (348 a). Paradoxically, however, Plato has given a solution to the dilemma I have outlined earlier about the impossibility of teaching either Theory or deconstruction as methods: if Plato disqualifies textuality as the realm of the uncertain, the site of a dangerous de-authorization, a constitutional lack of origin through which meanings can be twisted endlessly out of their contexts, he has proved the necessity of teaching. Even if it is with a text used as a pretext, teaching reintroduces that urge to test an issue to the best of one's capacities in a face-to-face situation. Besides, after Plato has rejected the sophistries of the rhetorical analyses of poems (the logical or rhetorical form of Simonides's text does not interest him; he wants to rush to the question: what is virtue for me now?) we cannot forget that he has entrusted his dialogical dramatization to a written text, his own dialogue, preserved well enough to trigger discussions well into the twenty-first century.

Theaters of Theory

In the pedagogical context outlined, we may conclude that it would be hasty to identify Derrida's position with that of Protagoras: he shares with Plato's Socrates two fundamental tenets: first, a belief that the most essential form of knowledge leading to absolute competence cannot be taught as a method; second, he too is primarily interested by the exploration of an uncertain frontier linking more than separating foundationalist investigations into the question of essence and relativist incommensurabilities. An astute critic of Derrida who also argues consistently in favor of relativism, Joseph Margolis, assesses deconstructionist strategies rather warily: "In effect, Derrida's strategy is to *use* the various forms of logocentric thought and language so as to uncover, by internal subversion, evidence of a breach of the necessary, the originary, the closed, the privileged, the certain, the totalized, the invariant, which is to say to enable our most comprehensive science to 'proclaim its limits.'"[12] What Margolis does not say is that the "limitation" of the claims of science to totality sends us back both to an appreciation of de-originated texts in a way that would be refused by Plato while suggesting the absolute need for a continued pedagogy of this process. Can literature thus reach any truth? Socrates would say no, since there is no truth outside what can be reached through a living dialogue. For Protagoras, there is no absolute truth at all, since one can disprove but not prove; criticism is the best exercise for the fine-tuning of these rhetorical "suspensions." The question of a "truth in literature" is not simply settled by a recourse to a "fictional truth" that would be of another order altogether than the truths we meet in the "real world."[13]

Perhaps, as Margolis suggests, it is necessary to go back and take a look at another founder of deconstruction, albeit in a slightly different mode: Heidegger. I will try to link the two difficult topics of Heidegger's critique of technology and of his commendation of poetic language. My justification for this gesture derives from Plato's dialogue, at least from the speech he puts in Protagoras's mouth. In the myth developed by the Sophist, Zeus entrusts Prometheus and Epimetheus with the task of endowing mortals with individual features or "powers." First, Epimetheus assigns physical advantages to each animal species, keeping a strict balance of powers as an objective, but completely forgetting human beings, who remain naked, weak, and destitute. Prometheus then gives them fire, stolen from Ephaestus, and technical skills stolen from Athena. Prometheus pays dearly for his kindness as we know, and these godly arts (agriculture, weaving, metallurgy) to which are added language and religion do not suffice anyway: Zeus has to send Hermes who adds "justice" to the previous package, so that men may be able to live together in a stable social organization. The myth accounts for the invention of *techne*, a term that blends "arts" and "techniques," but shows clearly that without justice, that is a universally shared political expertise, since the point of the story is that Zeus distributes this virtue evenly among all humans, technology is severely limited. Protagoras seems to imply that *techne* was bestowed before any social organization was dominant, and that its "wild" use contributed to a further scattering of human groups (Annaud's filming of Rosny's *La Guerre du feu* would be a good contribution to the debate). The rest of the dialogue will turn around granting or not granting the status of science to commonly shared virtues like courage, and the political awareness which includes justice. This is where Heidegger's meditation on technology could comes into play: reflecting on the common belief that technology would have been produced relatively late in the history of civilization, after say the several "industrial revolutions" we have known in the eighteenth and nineteenth centuries, it looks as if science had emerged slowly to be followed

110

by technology. We believe that to be "modern" today means being affected in all domains of our lives by a tentacular "technocracy," in a bewildering proliferation of machines and techniques that has outstripped the tardy pace of culture.

This is a mistake Heidegger wishes to dispel: for him, technology precedes science, is more fundamental than science since it gives science its real essence; therefore the inaugural separation between *episteme* and *techne* which seemed crucial for Plato and Aristotle needs to be revised. We have seen how Plato attempted to found philosophy by repudiating the "techniques" disseminated (and sold dearly) by the Sophists: Plato argues for the superior value of knowledge, a science available to those who devote their lives nobly to its attainment. As the *Phaedrus* made clear, writing is not absent from the list of dangerous techniques, especially as its unrestrained use risks endangering a living memory. For Heidegger, an inversion of Platonism is a prerequisite to any original engagement with thought, since technological thinking, pursued essentially through mathematical calculation, impels Western philosophy toward a forgetting of Being. This is what he calls the *Gestell* or "enframing," a difficult idiosyncratic term coined to suggest all at once "frame(work)," "collective ordering of items in a whole," and "production."[14] This word designates not technology as deployed through the world in all its manifestations but the essence of technology, which has nothing technological in itself. The planetary domination of technology seems absolute today, yet Heidegger is intent upon showing that this is merely the culmination of a process he squarely equates with metaphysics at least since Plato and Aristotle. His solution does not merely consist in a regressive hankering after the blessed time of the pre-Socratics, or in an elegiac lament over the ruthless exploitation of nature. There is some nostalgia, it is true, when he opposes the Rhine sung by Hölderlin and today's river dammed up in order to generate power: "But, it will be replied, the Rhine is still a river in the landscape, is it not? Perhaps. But how? In no other way than as an object on call for inspection by a tour group ordered there by the vacation industry."[15] What the Situationists used to call "the society of the spectacle" along with all attendant capitalistic exploitations are but manifestations of the ubiquitous *Gestell*. A forester who measures

111

felled timber in a wood is thus only "made subordinate to the order-ability of cellulose, which is then delivered to newspapers and illus-trated magazines."[16]

However, Heidegger's tone is not wholly melancholic: by a rather sudden reversal, he sees in the deployment of this metaphysical essence the seeds of salvation. He has shown that the absolute evil was condensed in technology. He draws on two lines by Hölderlin ("But where danger is, grows / The saving power also") and simi-larly decides to find a saving grace just where the highest danger lies. By going back to its own root and almost beyond it, technol-ogy is made to disclose its revealing and concealing gesture, and further yet, its deep complicity with poetic creation. "There was a time when it was not technology alone that bore the name *techne* . . . Once there was a time when the bringing-forth of the true into the beautiful was called *techne*. And the *poiesis* of the fine arts also was called *techne*."[17] Curiously, the conclusion to the "Question Concerning Technology" seems to duplicate in 1955 an analysis pursued in 1936 about poetry. In "Hölderlin and the Essence of Poetry," Heidegger starts from an apparent contradiction in Hölderlin's definitions of poetry: on the one hand, poetry is said to be "the most innocent of all occupations," but it is also described as a play with language, "the most dangerous of goods."[18] How can one reconcile these two antagonistic versions? First, by showing that if poetry looks like a harmless game with words it is a game that can have dreadful consequences, as evinced by Hölderlin's descent into madness. The poet is shown playing with language in such a way that this play "makes language possible," but in order to achieve this he had to dig down to the roots of its very impossibility. Then, following the poet's insight into his role as mediator between men and gods, whose lightning brings an excess of light and its coun-terpart, total darkness, poetry assumes its function as verbal bridge toward an unnameable real. In a paragraph that has been omitted from the English version, Heidegger defines poetry as "the original naming of the gods" before asking: "How do the gods speak?"[19] They speak through "hints" (*Winke*) and the poet's task is to catch these and to convey them to his people; it is in this task that poetry finds a sure foundation, a firm grounding. The gods have fled *and* they are coming: this is how Hölderlin expresses poetically not only the timeless historicity of the essence of poetry but also the essence of Theory.

For in another text dealing with Science almost contemporaneous with the previously quoted essay on Technology, Heidegger poses the question of the validity of a statement like "Science is the theory of the real."[20] He then launches into a long etymological examination of the word "theory" which concludes with a double Greek origin: *theoria* derives from *theorein* which calls up *thea*, the root of "theater," to evoke ideas of looking, glance, aspect, outward appearance. This theater of vision is where presence shows itself in its *eidos*, so that it is then known. The second root, *horao*, implies looking attentively, closely, slowly, taking one's time in the contemplation. Heidegger then explains how "theory" was the supreme mode of existence for philosophers like Plato and Aristotle. It is the main goal set for humanity at the end of the *Nichomachean Ethics*, for instance.[21] However, Heidegger, who marvels at the way the Greeks "thought out of their language,"[22] adds a third etymological derivation: *thea* and *orao* can be inflected to read *thea* and *ora* and thus suggest *Thea*, the goddess. Theory would in fact mean beholding the goddess *aletheia* or Truth, in a contemplation that "keeps watch" over truth. And then, for Heidegger, the very shift from the Greek root of Theory to a Latin world *contemplatio*, marked by Christian piety, entailed a great conceptual weakening with important consequences for modern science.

> The essence of theory as thought by the Greeks, which is ambiguous and from every perspective high and lofty, remains buried when today we speak of the theory of relativity in physics, of the theory of evolution in biology, of the cyclical theory in history, of the natural rights theory in jurisprudence. Nonetheless, within "theory," understood in the modern way, there yet steals the shadow of the old *theoria*. The former lives out of the latter, and indeed not only in the outwardly identifiable sense of historical dependency.[23]

Leaving Heidegger's almost untranslatable meditations on science and nature (the relatively common idiom *das Unumgängliches* has to be rendered in heavy English by "that which is not to be gotten around") – a point which should force us to reconsider the links between poetry, etymology, language, science, and theory – I would like to move to slightly more solid philological ground.

In her invaluable study of "Theoria" Hannelore Rausch has mapped out the various etymologies regrouped on the word, adding a very important layer of meaning curiously and symptomatically omitted by Heidegger.[24] For the Greeks, Theoria was primarily connected with the noun *theoros*, meaning first an "observer," a "spectator," someone who travels to see men and things; this is also an ambassador, an official witness sent by the city either to represent it as a special envoy to religious ceremonies, in order to request an oracle, or to participate in special gatherings like communal games. This pledged deputy would attest that important events had really taken place. The verb *theorein* was often used intransitively to convey this particular activity described in Plato's *Laws* as a crucial piece of public relations, since a given theoros's reputation would color the renown of a whole city, or as a way of enlarging the community's view through extensive travels, as in Aristophanes's *Wasps* when one character regrets that he has had no opportunity of traveling further than Paros as a "Theoros" (l. 1188). The meanings correctly ascertained by Heidegger, the religious sense suggesting a vision of gods and goddesses, and the visual–epistemological beholding activity, both converge in a function which is "political" in the strictest sense: the official representative who is sent as an eye-witness is more than a citizen on jury-duty; he is an ad hoc magistrate pledging his honor to the city's highest values; in his authorized gaze, everyday deeds will be integrated into a sacred "theater": there, things will be seen under their most essential aspect, so that they can then be recorded officially. Rausch has demonstrated conclusively that this meaning still adheres to the more philosophical usage found in Plato and Aristotle.

Why then did Heidegger ignore this social and political function? The answer is probably to be found in the structural homology I have sketched between a prewar mediation on lyrical poetry and a postwar critique of science and technology. In both analyses the last word is left to the poet; Hölderlin, the mad German poet who had gazed at the gods from too close, would therefore provide the archetype of the *theoros*. Thus, beholding or witnessing is in no way an innocent activity, it is fraught with danger, it battles with countless impossibilities. This is why Heidegger chooses to apply Hölderlin's famous lines to the poet (and possibly to himself):

> Can we still believe that Hölderlin is trapped in an empty and excessive self-contemplation owing to the lack of wordly content [*Weltfülle*]? Or do we recognize that this poet, because of an excess of impetus, poetically thinks through to the ground and center of being? It is to *Hölderlin* himself that we must apply the verse which he said of Oedipus in that late poem "In lovely blueness blooms . . .":
> Perhaps King Oedipus has
> One eye too many. (VI, 26)[25]

Is it because Theory has so much to do with the visible and the invisible? Theory is best described by oxymoronic couplings like "seeing blindness" or "blind insight" so as to collapse the fates of Tiresias the blind seer and Oedipus the blind tragic hero, both gathered under the aegis of a excessive epistemophilia. Accordingly Hans Blumenberg begins his fascinating account of the genealogy of Theory with the statement that "Theory is something that one does not see."[26] I have already mentioned Thales's fall and the feminine laughter that accompanies it, which suggests that Theory is always caught up between comedy and tragedy. No one knew this better than Nietzsche when he let Oedipus at Colonnus leave as his dying words this "Soliloquy of the Last Philosopher" inscribed to "the history of posterity":

> I call myself the last philosopher, because I am the last man. No one speaks with me but myself, and my voice comes to me like the voice of a dying man! . . . But the world continues to live and only stares at me even more glitteringly and coldly with its pitiless stars. It continues to live as dumbly and blindly as ever, and only *one thing* dies – man.[27]

Another aphorism on the same page suggests that art provides the only form of salvation: "The terrible loneliness of the last philosopher! Nature towers rigidly around him; vultures hover above him. And so he cries out to nature, 'Grant me forgetfulness!' *No, he endures suffering like a Titan until he is offered reconciliation in the highest tragic art.*"[28] Nevertheless it looks as if Prometheus and his dubious gifts of *techne* had finally replaced Oedipus.

4

Theory Not **of** *Literature But* **as** *Literature*

We may object: isn't it too easy to let an old unrepentant Nazi thinker like Heidegger give the last word in heavy pseudo-poetic prose on the serious issue of the links between science and literature? Isn't the privilege granted Nietzsche or Hölderlin too clearly an excuse for a political responsibility Heidegger himself never acknowledged? I would be the last to wish to exonerate him from a deep ethical failure facing monstrosities like fascism and the Final Solution. In that respect, however, Heidegger appears in a position similar to that of Céline or Ezra Pound, caught up between ethical demands for justice that they failed to observe and an epistemological desire to adhere fully to their time's unleashing of old demons. They are thus interesting not *in spite of* their weakness or pusillanimity, but *because* they allowed themselves to be traversed by the worst seductions in the name of a total "revolution" that had in fact returned to the most archaic reveries and prejudice. In this context, Adorno's declaration on the impossibility of lyrical poetry after Auschwitz has been too often quoted and misunderstood, which is why I prefer turning once more to Barthes for nuggets of wisdom. In a meditation on "literature as mathesis" he writes the following:

Reading classical texts (from *The Golden Ass* to Proust), he is always amazed by the sum of knowledge amassed and aired by the literary work . . . literature is a *mathesis*, an order, a system, a structured field of knowledge. But this field is not infinite: on the one hand, literature cannot transcend the knowledge of its period; and on the other, it cannot say everything: as language, as *finite* generality, it cannot account for objects, spectacles, events which would surprise it to the point of stupefying it; this is what Brecht sees when he says: "The events of Auschwitz, of the Warsaw ghetto, of Buchenwald certainly would not tolerate a description of literary character. Literature was not prepared for such events, and has not given itself the means to account for them."

Perhaps this explains our impotence to produce a realistic literature today: it is no longer possible to rewrite either Balzac, or Zola, or Proust, or even the bad socialist-realist novels, though their descriptions are based on a social division which still applies.[1]

Barthes concludes from this impotence (an impotence from which he was suffering in his own literary efforts, as we have seen, precisely because he could not repeat Proust and was not inclined toward experimental writing) that literature has lost its epistemic function; unable to be either *Mimesis* or *Mathesis* it is condemned to be pure *Semiosis*, signification unleashed from the need to represent a world or organize knowledge. The rapid transition from considerations of novelistic mathesis to an ethical difficulty in representing adequately unspeakable horror may appear a little brisk. One unresolved issue would then be to know whether literature still upholds a limited knowledge or none at all.

Theory's Price-Tags

This generates two related questions whose imbrication yields a further source of bafflement. First, if there is always a knowledge conveyed by literature, where does it reside? Is it simply that a good novelist somehow sums up a period whose objects, characters, and attitudes it embalms forever? Or that literature functions as repository for a culture's material world and a particular tradition's more ethereal values? Secondly, what kind of knowledge is needed to decipher the knowledge at work in literature? Should one trust mimesis and look to literature for a simple reflection of reality, following the old image of a mirror dragged along the way, so as to reconstruct nineteenth-century Paris with Balzac and Baudelaire, or rebuild turn-of-the-century Dublin with Joyce, or should one stress the relative autonomy of the work of art and concentrate on its formal properties? Can the two wishes be reconciled or is the alternative radical?

If Proust would probably agree that realism is no longer "possible" after a certain point in history, it might not be for the same reasons as Barthes. Besides, it is not so clear that he can be called a "classical novelist." Proust is indeed classical in the sense that he faithfully describes a society that is dying under his very eyes, and whose values he criticizes, but without endorsing the new tide of "popular" fiction. He would nevertheless concur with Barthes about the limitations of social realism — even if the genre was promoted as the only literature compatible with a revolutionary ideology by Stalinist doctrinaires like Zhdanov two decades after Proust's death, and if his novel embodies the culmination of the social documentary. Proust's ambivalence facing these issues is perceptible when he talks about literary or aesthetic theories. For him, novels that have theories in them are like gifts on which one has left the price-tag; the phrase is neat and often quoted, but it is worth giving its full context. This occurs in *Time Regained* after the great discovery of the "uneven paving stones" in the Guermantes courtyard: the narrator has seized a principle that will underpin the rest of his life, the possibility of finding an objective correlative linking the unconscious work of memory and sensory impressions: literature will just have to produce the juxtaposition by creating powerful metaphors that will enshrine things and feelings in a space free from Time. Proust has just launched a tirade against those who, especially after the Dreyfus affair and the Great War, have started denouncing the "ivory tower" in which artists have been imprisoned and, in the name of "life," exalt committed literature, finding humble subjects or noble causes that should at least be accessible to the masses. Proust seems to have a grudge against Romain Rolland in that particular passage:

And it is perhaps as much by the quality of his language as by the species of aesthetic theory which he advances that one may judge of the level to which a writer has attained in the moral and intellectual part of his work. Quality of language, however, is something the critical theorists think that they can do without, and those who admire them are easily persuaded that it is no proof of intellectual merit, for this is a thing which they cannot infer from the beauty of an image but can recognize only when they see it directly expressed. Hence the temptation for the writer to write intellectual works – a gross impropriety. A work in which there are theories is like an object which still has its price-tag on it. (And as to the choice of theme, a frivolous theme will serve as well as a serious one for a study of the laws of character, in the same way that a prosecutor can study the laws of anatomy as well in the body of an imbecile as in that of a man of talent, since the great moral laws, like the laws of the circulation of the blood or of renal elimination, vary scarcely at all with the intellectual merit of individuals.) A writer reasons, that is to say he goes astray, only when he has not the strength to force himself to make an impression pass through all the successive states which will culminate in its fixation, its expression. The reality that he has to express resides, as I now began to understand, not in the superficial appearance of his subject, but at a depth at which that appearance matters little; this truth had been symbolized for me by that clink of a spoon against a plate, that starched stiffness of a napkin, which had been of more value to me for my spiritual renewal than innumerable conversations of humanitarian or patriotic or internationalist or metaphysical kind. "Enough of style," had been the cry, enough of literature, let us have life![2]

As Malcolm Bowie and other commentators have shown,[3] such an attack on theories may strike readers as extremely paradoxical when it comes from a writer who develops theories about everything under the sun – *In Search of Lost Time* is known for its particular status as a "philosophical novel" in which the narrative is constantly impeded by the most varied theories on art, beauty, snobbism, jealousy, homosexuality, food, music, travels, drunkenness, memory, forgetting, perception, and what not. They range from short parenthetical asides like the one in the previous excerpt to longish developments that can take twenty pages. This is even truer of *Time Regained*, since it was to contain, according to the original plan of the book, a solution to all the riddles left dangling in the first part. And if we pay closer attention to the genesis of the novel, we may remember that Proust decided at a relatively late stage to include what he had planned hitherto as a separate treatise on homosexuality, the disquisition on "men-women" which makes up much of the bulk of *Sodom and Gomorrah* or *Cities of the Plain*, part one. These insertions or digressions make the reading more strenuous but contribute to the impression of "modernity" in this novelistic masterpiece.

Proust opposes here aesthetic theories to the "truths" or "laws" one discovers by chance, alone, in the simplest sensations that, ordered together, become like religious visitations. This is of course connected with the concept of involuntary memory, these "resurrections" which force us to discover truth in a fundamental passivity: the book we need to write is the book written in us by reality without our knowledge, in countless material traces left by the impact of sensations. This excludes by definition any literary program, any decision to choose "themes" that will be shared by all, since it is only by descending deep into oneself that one can excavate these buried privileged moments. The discovery leads by stages to a conclusion that is the direct opposite of the war-cry of the "theoreticians": at the end, the narrator discovers that real life is literature, that there is nothing more important that the creation of a work in which all these metaphors can be connected architectonically. Proust's often discussed and limited Bergsonism no doubt plays a part in this crusade against the superficiality of intelligence. The aesthetic theories expounded by writers and critics despised by Proust nevertheless remind him of his precarious position facing the social dimension of his work. He has to mobilize all his energies in a series of inchoate self-admonitions that finally lead the narrator to the decision of becoming a novelist. This can only happen because he has the strong conviction that he has found a truth, and that this truth will disclose universal laws which are similar to those of science (here medical science, a family specialty, is invoked for instance).

On the other hand, how are we to treat all the homemade "theories" that are scattered throughout the novel? One might say that each time the narrator reaches a "theory" – often introduced by a "as I now began to understand" as in the passage quoted – it describes merely a stage, a partial truth discovered on his way to a deeper and more comprehensive knowledge. In that sense, many theories expounded or, it seems, extemporized by the narrator on the smallest pretext would not fundamentally differ from those of a Leopold Bloom walking in Dublin and imagining that INRI on a crucifix means "Iron Nails Ran In," or that it was a nun who invented barbed wire.[4] They would not differ significantly either from what Freud called children's theories about sexuality: the various fantasies created by younger children who refuse to take in the facts of sexual difference and then invent plausible although often grotesque solutions like storks, anal births, or the idea of fecundating a woman through a kiss. Let us not forget that for Freud, these theories all answer to the fundamental riddle: "Where do children come from?" and all suppose an original solution – often by granting men and women a penis. By a bold jump, one may say that they all contain some element of truth – the truth that Freud tries to recapture with his theory of castration – and that this truth will echo in countless "myths and sagas" as Freud said.[5] This led Beckett to the savage aside in *The Unnamable* when he warned us against any kind of theory: "Enough of acting the infant who has been told so often how he was found under a cabbage that in the end he remembers the exact spot in the garden and the kind of life he led there before joining the family circle."[6] And Beckett knew exactly where to search in Proust's works, whose anti-intellectualism struck him as Romantic: it points toward a contemplation stripped of its usual reasons: "we are reminded of Schopenhauer's definition of the artistic procedure as 'the contemplation of the world independently of the principle of reason.' In this connection Proust can be related to Dostoevsky, who states his characters without explaining them."[7] Bakhtin's dialogism is therefore not very far, it still propels Theory along its paradoxical and devious path.

Thus we do not need to disparage Proust's theories in the name of his own caveat since they are all entirely necessary to the narrative; for instance, what appears as a mildly absurd denouement at the end, namely the fact that all the male and female characters of the novel with whom the narrator had engaged, with the exception of his family, are revealed to be "inverts," in short that they all are or have been homosexual, is accounted for in the analysis of "sodomy" disclosed much earlier. Therefore, if we pay closer attention to the sentence: "A writer reasons, that is to say he goes astray, only when he has not the strength to force himself to make an impression pass through all the successive states which will culminate in its fixation, its expression," it will be clear that the only theory that can be really valid is a theory that can account for the novel's production – a theory disclosed in the last pages of *Time Regained*. Following the etymological series we have investigated with Heidegger, the narrator will then be simultaneously a witness, an observer, and a theater of his own self: the theory will be indistinguishable from the narrator's subjective progression through other theories and other discoveries leading him step by step to a final epiphany and resolution to write. Thus an empirical progress (as we know, quite bumpy in Proust's case, since the war forced him to revise a text he thought almost completed, and made him change countless details) and the ideal scheme can fuse completely.

However, Proust's ambivalence facing theories should warn us not to be taken in by an idealizing gesture that would superpose the schema of Hegel's *Phenomenology of Spirit* and the novel. A genetic reading of *Time Regained* disposing of all the successive drafts ordered vertically in a hypertext would not only highlight several ruptures and inconsistencies – this would be too long to demonstrate here – but also point to important theoretical bifurcations in Proust's last volume. I will only refer to one of these here, the moment when the narrator decides to mention the real name of the cousins of Françoise (still a fictional character) who went out of their way to help a niece who was a war widow:

> In this book in which there is not a single incident which is not fictitious, not a single character who is a real person in disguise, in which everything has been invented by me in

accordance to my theme, I owe it to the credit of my country to say that only the millionaire cousins of Françoise who came out of retirement to help their niece when she was left without support, only they are real people who exist.[8]

No doubt the strong emotion one discerns here has been brought about by war tragedies; this forces not only a new ethical respect facing anonymous people but also triggers a rare outburst of nationalist fervor. Here, obviously, reality intrudes; it dismantles any fictional theory closed upon itself by contributing directly to a curious break in the novel's own codes. I will now turn to a rapid analysis of Joyce's work in the hope of discovering a similar pattern linking theory, *theoria*, and modernist textuality.

If Joyce's place in modernism appears today more fundamental than Proust's, it is not only because his works play the role of keystone in our current conceptions of modernism, but above all because he has acted more obviously as a logical attractor for all the various discourses and methods commonly deployed as Theory. His remarkable plasticity and adaptability can excite envy from scholars who have devoted their careers to less favored authors – after deconstructive, Lacanian, postcolonial, feminist, and new historicist waves, Irish nationalists, late Marxist or post-nationalists have followed suit; it looks as if all the recognized critical schools had elected his works as a privileged testing ground or dumping site. One already sells guides to visit these piles of layered discourses just as in *Finnegans Wake* a janitor, or rather a janitrix, will show you the Waterloo museum with this tip: "Penetrators are permitted into the museomound free."[9] In spite of this increased visibility (or should we say "visitability"?) we find as important a discrepancy between Joyce's textual practice and the theories that underpin the construction of his novels as with Proust. There is no doubt that Joyce can be taken as an example of the loaded relationship between modernism and Theory on the one hand, and between an author's "theories" about what he or she is doing and the very writing of fiction these theories are supposed to generate, on the other hand. Why is it that Joyce wrote enough critical essays to make up a volume of *Critical Writing* and then decided to abandon the idea of writing a self-contained aesthetic treatise? One may argue that for pragmatic reasons of writerly concentration, he refused to spend much time or energy in the kind of critical writing that gives the works of modernist contemporaries like Woolf, Pound, Lewis, or Eliot that useful horizon of secondary references and self-commentaries. Yet one needs to account for the discrepancy that arises between earlier texts like *Stephen Hero* in which the main protagonist is shown repeatedly flaunting an aesthetic theory in front of friends and adversaries, and later texts like *Ulysses*, from which similar theories are either taken as signs of immaturity or simply slowly fade before more important ethical values.

In his Dublin years, Joyce would assert that his mind worked better than those of gifted contemporaries like Yeats or Synge because he disposed of a rigorous theory when they were still dallying with Romanticism or late Symbolism, and that accordingly his collected works as envisioned *sub specie aeternitatis* were to be crowned by an aesthetic theory. The recurrent claim appears quite clearly in a letter sent in March 1903 to his mother by a Parisian exile who would soon return to Dublin at the news that she was dying of cancer. With juvenile bluster, Joyce outlines a work schedule covering the next decades: "Synge says I have a mind like Spinoza! . . . I am at present up to the neck in Aristotle's Metaphysics . . . My book of songs will be published in the Spring of 1907. My first comedy about five years later. My "Esthetic" about five years later again. (This *must* interest you!)."[10] Surprisingly, Joyce's boastful assertion and proud philosophical models (Spinoza and Aristotle, no less) contain a prediction that turned out almost right about the dates: *Chamber Music* was published in 1907, while *Exiles* (clearly a comedy, albeit of a very particular kind) is supposed to take place in the summer of 1912, and the first notes for the play date from around 1913. However, no "Esthetic" was ever published or written by Joyce, even if one puts together the reviews, newspapers articles, and political essays in his *Critical Writings*. If one added a few theoretical passages in *Ulysses* mostly culled from Stephen's ruminations on art, paternity, creation, and rhythm, one might transform Joyce's *oeuvre* into a theory-friendly whole. One could also select theoretical fragments from letters, reviews, and essays in the hope of reconstituting the coherence of an aesthetic system. Whatever its title might be, it should be subtitled "Toward an Aristotelian poetics," since in the same letter to his mother Joyce explains that he spends his days reading Aristotle in the Sainte Geneviève library opposite the Panthéon – surely keeping an eye on this Republican monument honoring the nation's "great men" while scanning with the other the thoughts of *'l maestro de color che sanno*.

The best point of entry into Joyce's shrinking theory should be *mimesis*, the Aristotelian concept that maps out the entire field of his revision of classical aesthetics.

Epiphanies of Theory

Mimesis does not just call up a crucial moment in Aristotle's *Poetics*, but by suggesting banal "imitation" in the sense of merely repro-ducing what one has seen or heard, it also underwrites the curious vanishing act played by the "epiphanies," a term which for most readers of the earlier novels and stories just condenses the whole of Joyce's aesthetics. The first definition of an epiphany betrays its mimetic nature when in *Stephen Hero* we see Stephen catching snatches of dialogue between a man and a woman in Eccles Street one misty evening. If it does not really make much sense for us, the fragment evokes a scene written for the stage:

> The Young Lady – (drawling discreetly) . . . O, yes . . . I was . . . at the . . . cha . . . pel . . .
> The Young Gentleman – (inaudibly) . . . I . . . (again inaudibly) . . . I . . .
> The Young Lady – (softly) . . . O . . . but you're . . . ve . . . ry . . . wick . . . ed . . .[11]

This is all, a disappointing dialogue in which dots and ellipses count more than what is said; from this, it seems that the epiphany defines a quintessentially Pinterian mode of dialogue that makes silence more significant than what is being said. In this case, the incident affects the budding poet's sensitivity and, what is more, gives him a model of literary task since he decides to collect similar items in a "book of epiphanies." A definition of the epiphany

126

follows: "a sudden spiritual manifestation, whether in the vulgarity of speech or of gesture or in a memorable phase of the mind itself."[12] The lack of content in the actual words of the vignette is constitutional and condenses a fascinating mixture of Irish paralysis and sexual innuendo, which moreover forces readers to be "wicked" in the place of the unnamed and apparently quite tame protagonists. Besides, this suggestive emptiness spreads: not only has it to be repeated so as to generate a serial concept, but it also points to a constitutive gap in language. Having captured less a moment of plenitude than a void in a voice or loopholes in dialogues, Stephen decides to compose a book made up of such cuts, swoons, and fadings.

This shows again how the link between two meanings of *theory* we have encountered so far can be productive – first, the capture by the reflecting mind of a moment of revelation in a privileged glimpse or audition, then, through the deliberate procession of these moments, the emergence of some order or process underpinned by a sense of "authority." We know from archival evidence and the testimony of friends that Joyce did collect these moments in a "book" of which he could legitimately claim to be the author, although it was never published. In the jagged path leading to self-authorization, epiphanies appear thus as snapshots caught at unforeseen intersections, Baudelairian beacons or lightning flashes in the dark night of urban *spleen*, Benjaminian illuminations catching a flickering aura among the myriad chance encounters with anonymous and troubling strangers seen or heard on the street. Trivialities indeed. Like the crazy and magical signs "invented" in the streets of Paris by Nadja in front of Breton's wonderstruck eyes, epiphanies happen when one lets the Real intrude at every street corner: the Real beckons, it is just a matter of capturing the sign it flashes. If Baltimore in the early dawn gave Lacan an image of the Unconscious, Eccles Street at dusk opened for Joyce similar vistas on the intimate interpenetration of signs, places, and people. Or to go back to Heidegger's evocation of a half-demented poet on the lookout for a god's "winks" (*Winke*), one might say that these lopped or truncated signs are displayed only in a corner (*Winkel*): not only at street-corners but also on the spot of the missing corner (as a blind spot, in other words) of a parallelogram in Euclid's "gnomon," that curious geometrical figure evoked at the beginning of the first story in *Dubliners*. Such a gap actually produces a knowledge of a particular kind, a private initiation to *gnosis* and of course endless textual glosses.

In the epiphanies as we know them today, forty vignettes survive out of the seventy-one numbered by Joyce, and they evince great variety. The short texts range between dream transcriptions, fragments of dialogues, first drafts of objective narratives, and lyrical autobiographical confessions. The impression left by these fragments on their author must have been strong indeed, since most of these already written passages reappear throughout the later fiction: *A Portrait of the Artist as a Young Man* is built upon twelve important epiphanies, spanning the trajectory from the first scene evoking castrating eagles (already the first epiphany) to the last page in which another epiphany, number thirty, salutes life and the "spell of arms and voices." A few other epiphanies recur with a curious and inexplicable insistence throughout all of Joyce's works. These texts seem to play the function of a computer's Index, like keyed prompters needed to retrieve files that have been distributed randomly in a disk. Enigmatic as they may be, these recurrences should not veil another factor: when these pre-written fragments are reintroduced into all the novels' narrative texture, they lose their own status as epiphanies, they just merge into pure text. This is why the term is not even mentioned in *A Portrait of the Artist as a Young Man*, whereas it has clearly become derogatory in *Ulysses* (Stephen muses in ironic retrospection on his juvenile fantasy of sending copies of his "epiphanies on green oval leaves" to "all the great libraries of the world, including Alexandria").[13] Is it that by the late 1910s Joyce no longer believed in his theory of the epiphany? Or is it that the term has already been swallowed by a generalized mimesis at work in the writing itself?

To try to answer this last question, one may note that the epiphany does not define a type of writing: if epiphanies have a format, roughly shorter than a Romantic prose-poem, generally not more than half a page, they have no style or genre of their own. "Style" has been devoured by "writing," as Barthes would have it, and this writing is devoured by the exterior or inner stage; this finally leads to an interactive process: object and subject are connected in such a way that one keeps hesitating between these poles. If, for the Stephen of *Stephen Hero*, "the clock of the Ballast office was capable of an epiphany,"[14] *a fortiori* any object will be "capable" of a similar process of inner and outer illumination. Aesthetic pleasure in this case derives from one's ability to prolong the hesitation, a hesitation that is all the more palpable as we balance between a religious and a profane sense of the term. The Dublin clock allegorizes epiphanies in Stephen's technological version of the theory in such a way that a gigantic spiritual camera seems at work behind his aesthetics: "Imagine my glimpses at that clock as the gropings of a spiritual eye which seeks to adjust its vision to an exact focus. The moment the focus is reached the object is epiphanised. It is just in this epiphany that I find the third, the supreme quality of beauty."[15] Whenever the subjective pole is downplayed, it is in the name of a forthcoming general theory of art. Stephen follows suit with an attack on tradition after which he quotes and distorts Aquinas's three concepts of "integrity," "wholeness," and "radiance" in support of his theory.[16] If the epiphany manifests the very soul of an object met or found in an overwhelming flash of insight, it is because it underpins a principle of individuation comparable to Duns Scotus's "haecceitas" (especially revisited by Hopkins): the absolute singularity shines forth so as to prove the existence of a God in love with "dappled" things. Joyce has chosen Aquinas as a guide but is not above gross distortions – thus Stephen unscrupulously replaces the "good" by the "true" in his discussions of beauty. Moreover he is careful to disentangle his line of reasoning from a theological system based upon the notion of divine and human love.

True, Joyce was not Hopkins, although he had studied in the same university, and he soon got rid of the Platonic and Romantic echoes still lurking in the first version of his theory when he rewrote *Stephen Hero*. In *A Portrait of the Artist as a Young Man* the same phraseology recurs without being founded on the term of "epiphany." This has the effect of making readers follow Stephen's "curve of an emotion" while seeing the elaboration of the theory of epiphanies as a mere stage, a progression through juvenile neo-Shelleyian aesthetics. This is confirmed by the fact that if the novella "The Dead" which concludes *Dubliners* takes place around the Epiphany, the "manifestation" showing forth the divine nature of

Jesus brings a final disclosure to be sure, but rather in the negative rather than in the positive: Gabriel does not carry "good news" for anyone but squarely confronts his own blindness, his male selfishness and emotional limitations. Like Stephen who brags about a "theory" concocted through an Aquinas whom he does not understand fully, Gabriel's discovery of his own limits facing a wife who emerges as a more and more opaque "other" for him leads to a radical revision of all his values; there is therefore a narrative process at work which is more crucial than the perception of the radiance of the thing qua thing because it forces an ethical revision of the subject qua subject. The subjective pole had not been forgotten, it was just eclipsed for a while by the theory before returning with a vengeance like the Freudian repressed it concealed.

ethical

While showing the radiance of manifestation, epiphanies do not conceal their own blindness; this is why the term keeps the important connotation of "betraying." By revealing something that had been concealed, the epiphany condenses a whole process of *aletheia*, that is truth as unconcealment, in a movement parallel to Benjamin's dialectic of "auras" and "traces" we have already encountered. Joyce's epiphany is never far either from the Freudian symptom or from the political drama of an Ireland endlessly abused and betrayed. In his brother Stanislaus's account, the "manifestations or revelations" in which the epiphanies consist undo the very process of ideological concealment while exhibiting ironically the type of repression at work: "these notes were in the beginning ironical observations of slips, and little errors and gestures – mere straws in the wind – by which people betrayed the very things they were most careful to conceal."[17] In epiphany no. 12, for instance, we see Hanna Sheehy, asked who is her favorite German poet, reply sententiously after a pause and a hush: "I think . . . Goethe . . ." This very Proustian irony derives from the multiplication of dots. It is a true epiphany because the pretensions of a shallow culture taking itself too seriously, in a word "provincialism," have been revealed through a condensation of personal, social, and cultural symptoms. In brief, the epiphany is not the key (given in the first drafts and then withheld for obscure reasons) of a theory of aesthetics but a bridge to a mimetic practice of language. It is all the more important to understand what Joyce means by mimesis.

130

In the Paris notebook (1903) one often quoted entry comments on Aristotle: "*e tekhne mimeitai ten physin* – This phrase is falsely rendered as 'Art is an imitation of Nature.' Aristotle does not here define art; he says only, 'Art imitates Nature' and means here that the artistic process is like the natural process."[18] Joyce transforms a noun into a verb in order to present mimesis as a process connecting art with life and to refuse any divorce between them. This idea recurs in Joyce's aesthetics, from the very early essay "Drama and Life" (1900) that urges following the model of Ibsen who has "let fresh air in,"[19] to a declaration made to an Irish friend after *Ulysses* had been published: ". . . that is now what interests me most, to get to the residuum of truth about life, instead of puffing it up with romanticism, which is a fundamentally false attitude."[20] Joyce stubbornly resists a Romanticism always associated with lyrical delusion. Ibsen, whom Joyce took as his first literary model, is superior even to Shakespeare because he grapples with real life in all its aspects, including politics and feminism.

Once more, this position can claim Aristotle as a source of inspiration. If *Poetics* defines tragic drama as the "imitation of an action" that produces pity and terror, it is because the playwright's aim is not the creation of a resembling picture of this or that man, but triggers emotions akin to those expressed by suffering characters like Oedipus. Butcher's commentary on Aristotle's *Poetics*[21] (a book upon which Joyce based his remarks, as Aubert and Schork have demonstrated)[22] insists upon the idea that mimesis is the imitation of an action, that is of real "men in action." This is why music and dancing can be said to "imitate" passions – a far cry from any "classical realism" in the novel. Butcher concludes that "imitation" is synonymous with "producing" or "creating according to a true idea,"[23] which suggests a dynamic theory of an imitation linked with a living process completely divorced from any preconception of the beautiful. Joyce's itinerary from Aristotle to Vico appears thus relatively direct, since both philosophers share the belief that imitation is a fundamentally human process and not based upon any notion of the beautiful or even limited to categories of aesthetics. Obviously, Joyce's concept of imitation is Aristotelian and not Platonic and its realism is psychological or biological not ontological or essential, which has important consequences. Stephen explains at one point

131

that "Aristotle's entire system of philosophy rests upon his book of psychology."[24] Accordingly, Joyce's effort will be to parallel the formal structures of the work of art with the stages of the mind's apprehension of beautiful things. It follows that psychology and aesthetics are both underwritten by a more fundamental genetic and mimetic rationality; as with Proust, therefore, aesthetics cannot be a "science of the particular," a *mathesis singularis*, without providing the general laws that account for its own genesis. But in the very process, aesthetic theory disappears as such to let textuality reign supreme. No price tag remains on the beautiful vase, all the tags have become leaflets and *paperoles* flushing out an ever expanding textual archive.

In *Stephen Hero* the youthful Stephen Dedalus was portrayed as a hero above all because he managed to link the production of an aesthetic theory with an attitude of refusal or subversion of dominant bourgeois values. This was accompanied by an attendant fetishization of the word "theory," the term being a short-cut for "aesthetic theory" but brandished in a repeated gesture of distanciation and negation, but also of ecstatic contemplation leading to a heightened sense of revelation – as when Stephen is described exultant, under the shock of the vision of a young girl wading in the sea at the end of chapter 4 in *A Portrait of the Artist as a Young Man*. The Aristotelian heritage claimed by Joyce led him to refuse any separation between beauty and life; can this push him closer to a concept of the sublime? This is what Ginette Verstraete has argued when she introduced the idea of a "feminine sublime" based less on Kant or Hegel than on Schlegel's aesthetics.[25] If the concept of the "feminine sublime" is relevant, it is because it encompasses ugliness and ridicule. Thus even if Joyce was perhaps not cognizant of Schlegel's theses, he shares with him an insight into the duplicity, irony, and reversibility of any gendered version of the sublime. On the whole, Joyce felt the need to move beyond the confines of German Romanticism, whether under its neo-Hegelian contribution with Bosanquet, or under Schlegelian guises, so as to engage less with weaker offshoots of Hegelianism than with earlier forms of "philosophy of history." History would turn into the single locus for a mimesis that could not be measured by subjective psychological categories alone, or of a sublime that tended to overthrow all the older forms determined by previous representations.

Thus Joyce deliberately regressed from Hegelianized theories of History to Vico's *ricorsi storici* in the *New Science*. Vico becomes his favorite source of inspiration because his aesthetic theories like the investigations into the "true Homer" or the theories of a "poetic language" made up by bodily metaphors cannot be distinguished from his theory of the cyclical return of cultures and civilizations. In Vico, Joyce found another version of the Aristotelian notion of mimesis as a congenital property of men's activities in the world. The concept of mimesis could then be reinterpreted according to what is, for Vico, the world of civil society. It is in fact for him the only world that we can ever know, since we cannot fathom the world of absolute truths residing in God only, the world of historical and social artifacts kept in archives, monuments, and living language. In Vico's account of the genesis of language, the archaic giants who had thus far been sporting in the open evolved a mimetic response to the noise of the thunder, a noise interpreted (which gives us the date of the invention of hermeneutics) as God's rebuke facing sexual license. These primitive beings then took refuge in caves, where they had leisure to devise marriage ceremonies, funerary rituals, and scribal writing in order to keep records of kinship lines. The first men, acting like children prone to imitating everything, also gave birth to our distinctively human and political culture. It is the epic of a historical process made up of such slow revolutions that is being narrated in *Finnegans Wake*.

Joyce's mimetic theory finally returns to the very old dream of a universal language. As Joyce was toiling on his "Work in Progress" for seventeen years, he found an unforeseen ally in a French Jesuit, Father Jousse. Jousse had started by investigating what he called the "rhythmico–motor" style perfected by a historicized Jesus in the tradition of Renan's *Life of Jesus*. Jousse's Jesus was a Rabbi teaching in such a way that his words would never be forgotten, exploiting all the resources of an embodied memory linked to the brain and the skeleton. This looked as a belated confirmation of Joyce's earlier theories about rhythm and language; in the "Trieste Notebook" one finds under the heading of "Esthetic" entries like "The skeleton conditions the esthetic image " and "Art has the gift of tongues." In *Ulysses* Stephen enters the red light district and exclaims: "So that gesture, not music not odours, would be a universal language, the gift of tongues rendering visible not the lay sense but the first entelechy, the structural rhythm."[26] Joyce reaches a satisfactory if incomplete theory of language through Stephen's divagations, while providing a basis for the construction of the tower of Babel of *Finnegans Wake.* Jousse's idea of a rhythmic verbo-motricity based on the bilateral nature of the body and the brain confirms earlier speculations on the silent language of gesture and the principle of a basic rhythm underpinning Universal History. Thus the language of the *Wake* is mimetic throughout, from lisping "baby talk" with Issy to Freudian symptoms betraying lust or hunger in Shaun's absurdly greedy speeches, while the human body provides the founding site for poetic metaphors leading to the utopia of a synthetic universal language.

Prostheses and Physiognomies

My two examples, Joyce and Proust, should lead us to ask a general question: as we have seen, monuments of modernism tend to include the theory of their production in such a way that it will not be visible any more, or even acknowledged by the author. Can one generalize this predicament, or is it only due to specifically modernist tactics and agendas? For a critic like Paul de Man, the paradigm should apply to all strong texts, since there is no way one could arrest the movement either chronologically (with distinctions between the Classics and the Moderns, say) or generically: any text, be it a poem, a novel, or hybrid production, will tend to include a philosophy of its own construction and therefore of its own rhetorical and philosophical deconstruction. One has not forgotten De Man's brilliant demonstration that Derrida's critical reading of Rousseau's alleged logocentrism not only presupposed issues of origins and authority his own theses were debunking, but also was blind to the way Rousseau's texts on language contained and per-formed a radical subversion of logocentrism.[27] On the other hand, for a critic like Milan Kundera, also a renowned novelist, the situ-ation has to be historicized and limited to the genre of the novel.[28] Only the novel can keep alive the long "European" (which for

Kundera as for Hegel includes the United States) tradition of dealing with a totality of life by recreating a whole world, albeit critically. Science increases a sense of splintering and dissociations of the universe in separate and self-contained discourses; the novel is the only site able to fulfill what Austrian novelist Hermann Broch had called "the impatience of knowledge." Broch knew, however, that he was writing "after" Joyce, Proust, and Kafka – then and only then would the need for some theory justifying philosophically or ethically the text's existence be felt.

Kundera sends us to Hermann Broch as a precursor, as the novelist and philosopher who did most to promote the age of a new "theoretical novel." This is exemplified in Broch's trilogy *The Sleepwalkers*, in which he claims to have invented a new form of narrative, the "theoretical novel" (*der erkenntnistheoretischer Roman*), which both leaves behind all "psychological novels" and completes the work of encyclopedic summation begun with *Ulysses*. Broch proudly confided to Mrs. Brody in 1930 that his own awe facing Joyce had made him miss at first the radical novelty of his method. What does the term imply? In the third volume of the *Sleepwalkers*[29] one finds interspersed in the many strands of narrative a lengthy and abstract philosophical essay divided into ten installments and entitled "Degradation of Values." They sketch a very mixed rag-bag of notions that revolve around the new predicament of the European spirit after a war that has unleashed mass destruction and mass psychosis; the belief in "reality" has been lost, as well as the foundation of values, the subjective "position of position" that mediates between personal irrational impulses and the "Platonic Logos" that each epoch formulates differently. Other digressions deal with architecture and ornament, with the autonomy of values-systems, and the increasing specialization of life and science, which entails discussions of logical positivism, theses by Kant, Hegel, and Kierkegaard, Marxism and revolutions, the recurrent leitmotif that art annihilates Time to spatialize life, and finally a whole theory of the *Zeitgeist* as deducible from the "style of an epoch." I only sketch these ideas so as to give a glimpse of what Broch calls "theory of knowledge" (*Erkenntnistheorie*), not to be confused with a general scientific epistemology (*Wissenschaftstheorie*). His main contention is that the novel today provides the only space for the reconciliation of ethics and aesthetics, and since science is so slow and compart-mentalized, for a vision of totality. The ethical impulse consists in bringing literature as close as possible to a form of knowledge in the making. Broch hopes to achieve this by bridging the gap between the personal–lyrical mode, general historical–ideological problematics of history and a metaphysical–logical thinking capable of discussing the various calculations of the "infinite" in different epistemological configurations.

What is remarkable is that the trilogy works even when one does not subscribe to all these theses and ideas; besides, Broch is clever enough to ascribe most of them to one character, a philosopher living in Berlin after the war; however, since the tenth "digression" is the novel's epilogue, they have to be considered as the author's opinion as well. What Broch offers as a new discourse for the novel (a path followed by few novelists, with rare exceptions like Musil, Pynchon, and Michel Rio) is to treat knowledge seriously. Broch was a mathematician and a philosopher whose idiosyncratic discus-sions of Husserlian phenomenology, logical positivism, and Hegelian philosophy of history are invaluable contributions. His work on political theory and mass psychosis in the 1950s is also quite impres-sive. The immediate impact on fiction (on Kundera at least) is con-siderable, since it allows the novelist to work without psychology in the traditional sense. The theoretical novel replaces traditional psychology of characters by value centers still individualized enough to be convincing, but close enough to theoretical modelizations.

What happens nevertheless when the same claim to knowledge is made in the name of Theory but with a Bakhtinian double-voicedness or a total lack of seriousness? Bakhtin has convinced us that the novel as a genre belongs to the tradition of Menippean satire which examines ideas more under the mode of farce and parody than as sedate intellectual discussion. After all Don Quixote is a hero who just happens to develop strange "theories" about mills and knights! This is where we need to return to the fate of Theory when it is greeted by laughter. The famous story of Thales's fall is best narrated in Plato's *Theaetetus* when Socrates refers to "the story about the Thracian maidservant who exercised her wit at the expense of Thales, when he was looking up to study the stars and tumbled down a well. She scoffed at him for being so eager to know what was happening in the sky that he could not see what lay at his feet."[30] Socrates then concludes with a bitter generalization: "Anyone who gives his life to philosophy is open to such mockery" (174 a). He then proceeds to expatiate on the philosopher's helplessness in practical matters of everyday life – to such a point that the philosopher cannot even walk normally: "when he is forced to talk about what lies at his feet or is before his eyes, the whole rabble will join the maidservants in laughing at him, as from inexperience he walks blindly and stumbles into every pitfall" (174 c).

Plato takes Thales as an emblem of this peculiar infirmity which derives from speculation and purely theoretical knowledge because Thales was the first "philosopher" or Sage registered by the Greek tradition, and because he offered bold hypotheses about the world (essentially made up of water, according to him) and the stars (he measured them, gave them the names of the constellations, wrote about equinoxes and solstices). The dangers and pleasures of pure speculation are underlined by Plato in a neat reversal: when the common man is brought to dizzying heights by the questioning of the philosopher, asking "What is justice?" for instance, then it will be his turn to be "dizzy from hanging at such an unaccustomed height and looking down from mid-air" (175 d). As Hans Blumenberg has demonstrated in his brilliant book *The Laugh of the Thracian Maid*, the long tradition of commentaries on the fall of the philosopher who looks up to the sky but cannot see the earth (it was narrated by Chaucer and Montaigne) should not be taken as a straightforward allegory of Theory's vulnerability.[31] While Heidegger kept returning to the anecdote (as in "The Question toward the Thing") in order to argue that science and philosophy should part their ways radically, Blumenberg tries on the other hand to reconcile them, accepting laughter for its corrective or sanitive properties, since this laughter spares nobody in the end.

In a similar vein, Balzac mocks the pretensions of contemporary science while producing his own science in his witty *Theory of the Walk*. This extravaganza published in 1833 displays its own rhetorical pyrotechnics by shrilly claiming to revolutionize knowledge; the narrator, similar to Poe's metaphysical cranks possessed by a "fixed idea," insists that this new "Théorie de la démarche" – the phrase

is repeated on almost every page – is a new blend of acute sociological observation and metaphysical deductions. He is accordingly
a little crazy ("This theory could only have been invented by a man
who is bold enough to come close to madness without fear, and
close to science without terror"),[32] but his genius is not devoid of
its Foucauldian moments of insight: he observes in order to class
and codify, to formalize the "code of walking" which is in fact a
key to social appearance. A number of aphorisms are produced
("The walk is the body's physiognomy," "rest is the body's silence,"
"grace requires round gestures," "when they walk, women can show
everything provided they do not let anything be seen"). The double
focus is an analysis of the body in movement and the production
of a social corpus through attitudes and dress codes. Fieldwork is
limited: once the narrator has grasped his principle, he just spends
one day on a boulevard observing all the Parisians who happen to
pass in front of him. This is a Benjamin's Balzac giving us a useful
social physiognomy from the point of view of the street *flâneur*
doubled by a comic observer who exploits the discourse of pseudo-
science as a repertoire of tricks and phrases; terms like "thesis,"
"axiom," "principle," "law," "treatise," "physiology," "truth," and
"study" recur emphatically.

Exactly contemporary with Carlyle's *Sartor Resartus*, this essay
occasionally turns into the zesty "theories of everything" that the
Romantics would love, and these include clothes and their various
allegorizations as social signs. Moreover, the French word *démarche*
keeps its crucial polysemy: it means gait and walk but also step,
move, progress, and method! In this delinquent method verging on
madness, one never forgets the old meaning of *theoria* as "procession of men and women in a city." Like Teufelsdröckh's chaos of
manuscripts taking off from all forms of vestments and investments,
the essay does not avoid clutter or glibness. I wanted nevertheless
to quote Balzac's physiologies and physiognomies not only as a
textual trace of a recurring risk whenever texts turn into theories
– a risk to which Proust has already warned us: the danger is less
pseudo-science than bad taste, especially if the text provides tips for
men and women who want to be successful and fashionable[33] – but
also as an argument that particular sciences that have lost their validity (think of Hegel's fascination for phrenology, physiognomy, astrol-

ogy, and palmistry) remain as literature. What both Plato and Hegel assert is the idea that ambivalence and paradoxes reign as long as natural phenomena are not accounted for by a theory – which is why Hegel concludes a long discussion of the bumps on skulls that may or may not account for a murderer's disposition by launching a parallel full of humor; he proves that Spirit may well ignore itself if it is reduced to being "only a bone" in "the same conjunction of the high and the low which, in the living being, Nature naively expresses when it combines the organ of its highest fulfillment, the organ of generation, with the organ of urination."[34] Conversely, to expand the theme of the "jokes of Nature," Schopenhauer would merely note that all the flowers we take as demure symbols of grace and delicacy are just sexual organs displayed in full view. Nature's naivety is such that we often forget to veil it with our own infantile sexual theories.

This disquisition on theories and physiognomies could also explain why Broch's trilogy opens with a spectacular close-up on one character's gait or walk. In the first page, we meet Herr von Pasenow, the old landowner whose son Joachim is the anti-hero of *The Romantic*, the first part of the trilogy, in a very striking fashion. He is described walking in Berlin from a perspective that is so critical and antagonistic that it soon dawns on us that the author must be putting into action his principle of "a position of position," that is of implying the point of view of a "narrator as idea" in each scene. Herr von Pasenow, who does nothing more here than walk in the streets to meet his son, triggers "extraordinary and inexplicable revulsion" in all those who cross him; they immediately associate him with the "slightly hysterical and yet arrogant aggressiveness which is often characteristic of small men."[35] Such hysteria is contagious: "yet one can quite well imagine some young man, blinded with hatred, hurrying back to thrust his cane between the legs of any man who walked in that way, so as to bring him down by hook or by crook and break his legs and put an end for ever to such a style of walking."[36] Reduced as he is to a devil's cake-walk or to the sinister ambling of a "dog on three legs," we may guess that some Oedipal drama is at work – since we have been forced into the position of revengeful son eager to show the length of his stick to the evil father – but happily we will be spared its theory. Or rather let us assume that Theory is like this cane, less useful to walk with than to trip an ugly old man who inspires sudden and irrational murderous urges. If, according to the Sphinx's riddle, we begin by walking on all fours and end by walking on three legs, the desired reconciliation of text and theory, the fusion between method, gait, and cane will only take place in old age. Who knew that the owl of Minerva was in need of a prosthesis?

There are indeed moments when the knowledge imparted by a novel bypasses the cumbersome dialect of the intellectual metalanguage. The quest for a "theory of the novel" provided by novels themselves, the search for a theory of literature immanent to literature, has led us to a dilemma: Theory aims at the most general questions, at a philosophical questioning of "totalities" positing, as Broch thought, a "Platonic logos," but it cannot avoid being enmeshed in the letter of the text, in partly untranslatable signifiers, in the intractably entangled network of private and historical allusions without which literature would not open up on to *mathesis singularis*, in other words, to theorizing in particular.

Conclusion

Hermann Broch's polymorphous *oeuvre* is the opposite of the perverse: it reminds us that Theory does not necessarily kill either textual enjoyment or textual production, and that, like the genre of the novel itself, it remains alert to its ethical, political, and historical responsibility. However, Broch almost stopped writing fiction in the last years of his life, so intent was he upon completing an ambitious theory of totalitarianism which impressed Hannah Arendt, positing the need to analyze mass psychosis and "crepuscular states" in order to prevent a return to Nazi dementia. For him, the standards of science and theory had higher value than fiction writing, yet the paradox is that Broch is remembered for his novels and plays only. There is a real (if relative and often revised) "immortality" – to quote Kundera once more – in works of art that often eludes scientists. Science is necessary to Theory but literature cannot be forgotten – if only as the surest means not to be forgotten.

Since I devoted parts of the last chapter to readings of Proust and Joyce, it is high time to note that today Proust and Joyce specialists have had to adapt to textual studies, genetic approaches, or manuscript scrutiny in such a way that the opposition between High Theory and literary history still upheld by Paul de Man in his *Resistance to Theory* seems to have lost much of its edge. Since I believe in a possible historicization of Theory in the name of my Balzacian Hysteria Principle (in his uniquely insightful *Journal of an Airman* Auden opened other avenues of inquiry by noting other varieties of "enemy walk" like the grandiose stunt, the melancholic stagger, and the paranoid sidle to which one could add the hysterical fall-and-bounce and the proletarian swagger),[1] it is clear that a simple chronological and institutional logic is at work there. The baby-boomers of Theory, that generation of scholars who, in France and Germany especially, had been burnt out by avant-garde Freudo-Marxism distilled by the Theory of the Text, found another niche in the early 1980s when the school of *critique génétique* fully emerged. Its claim to science was the dispassionate study of drafts and manuscripts of modern and contemporary authors; beginning with Heine, Hölderlin, Kafka, Stendhal, Balzac, Hugo, Flaubert, Zola, and Proust, it soon expanded to include Joyce, Eliot, Valéry, Aragon, Breton, Musil, Claudel, Benn, Woolf, Morris, and finally any author whose collected works would include either drafts or variants in the printed texts. The dynamic process of writing was expanded in both directions, since it would now include all pre-publication materials and all post-publication stages, like limited first editions, censored chapters, annotations or errors in successive editions (subsequently Dickinson, Whitman, and Pound have been successfully incorporated into the corpus of writers in need of such reorganization). Jerome McGann has been one of the most vocal American geneticians, while the incredible success story of the ITEM group in France has triggered various critical responses in Anglo-Saxon countries.[2] The complex state of some modernist works like Proust's, Pound's, or Joyce's has forced readers to become geneticians: no student of Moderns can ignore the controversies surrounding Gabler's publication of a new and revised text of *Ulysses* in 1984.

Let us not forget that, after Poe's groundbreaking "Philosophy of Composition" and Valéry's *Tel Quel*, an alleged structuralist like Barthes could also announce the age of genetic criticism when he pleaded for a History of Writing in 1953, developing on the occasion an interesting chemical metaphor: "Any written trace precipitates, as inside a chemical at first transparent, innocent and neutral, mere duration gradually reveals in suspension a whole past of increasing density, like a cryptogram."[3] Thus baby Barthes was not thrown away with the soiled waters of Theory by geneticians but tapped for his wealth of subtle strategies. In fact, genetic criticism did not abandon literary theory, but its object became more material, tangible, layered, as documentary traces in an archive. Nevertheless, it would be naive to assume that archives disclose their treasures at first glance: any genetic material has to be painstakingly constructed. This seems a logical step in the effort to combine hermeneutics and scientific methods; moreover, linguistics have not been evacuated,[4] but the old dominant model which accounted for some strengths and many weaknesses in structuralism has been refined and will not be taken as a universal paradigm. We have seen how Theory has always been haunted by a myth of the "hard sciences" so as to provide a respectable basis for true knowledge, while in fact these models have provided only trendy metaphors. If Sokal and Bricmont err when they believe that factual misrepresentations of the hard sciences totally disqualify the work of philosophers who use them in passing (should we say that Hegel's system is false because he got the number of planets wrong?), some hopelessly muddled passages by Deleuze, Guattari, or others make for painful or unintentionally funny reading.[5] Let us throw a veil of oblivion on such misguided efforts at letting hysteria and science converge.

However, it looks today as if the only scientific method available is what historians know quite well: the patient discipline of deciphering archives. What matters above all is the rigor of one's critical discourse, since it cannot be defined by an object, be it "material" as with drafts, archives, or variants, or more obviously constructed as when we talk of gender, race, or communities. Such rigor will then create a rhetorical space that will make its terms available and debatable for a wider interpretive community. More than scientists (who when they try to explain what they are doing often sound like poets or madmen for the uninitiated) an example could be found in contemporary artists who "play" at being scientists and mime scientific processes – suggesting like John Cage or Bill Anastasi that the only science that matters is Alfred Jarry's pataphysics (the science of imaginary problems and imaginary solutions) when applied to the twenty-first century.

Indeed, pataphysics often provides the most adequate description for what passes as current pedagogy of literary theory, especially if one works with the proliferating anthologies or critical guides already discussed. Often, the chronologies are sadly off-key, so-called schools slice through critical corpuses that really overlap, the usual suspects follow each other in a line-up suggesting that one always recognizes the last one as the killer. The most common set-up develops linearly with a list of schools, in which Formalism, Structuralism, Psychoanalysis, Marxism, and Poststructuralism are commonly relayed by Deconstruction, Feminism, Gender Studies, Queer Theory, New Historicism, Ethnic Studies, and Postcolonial studies to culminate with today's or possibly yesterday's "Cultural studies." In a totally distorted historicity foisted on the reader as Necessity, any hybrid turns meaningless. Besides, one gathers that Theory's bad name is blamed on deconstruction: deconstruction would have begun the splintering process leading to all subsequent assertions of the marginal in the name of alterity – whether the responsibility of embodying otherness falls to women, ethnic minorities, gays, lesbians, subalterns of any type, emerging cultures caught before any Westernization. All the hyphenated citizens, all the disenfranchised of the world, can join in the fray; as the excluded ones they have to be recuperated and promoted as crucial exceptions to the rule, in an endless game articulating center and margins, well described by Derrida as early as 1966.[6] Not only is the move dangerously regressive because it forces us to rely on identity politics, but potentially absurd – the hyphenation process is virtually endless, I am always more than just Irish-American-Polish or Franco-Belgian-Jewish. How far back should we go, of how many grandparents each endowed with special virtues can we boast, if we want to account for our uniquely specialized idiosyncrasies? At the opposite extreme, new historicism and cultural studies eschew either subversive decenterings or "elitist" treatments of literature by capitalizing on the enjoyment one never fails to derive from popular culture and reductive sociological generalizations.

While this hackneyed plot retains some relevance today, the sordid truth is that we have run out of "marginalized others" to use as conceptual levers for the dislocations of Theory. One has heard of reputed critics who have invested in dogs and cats, pathetically pandering to the urge to redeem the underdog; I myself can confess that I briefly entertained the idea of launching a "lice" school of Joyce criticism. If Mark Shell has dealt brilliantly with bulls, domestic pets, and all sorts of non-humans in his superbly free-ranging

Children of the Earth,[7] aliens (with numerous spin-offs in the abduction genre), parasites (it should be easy to find sponsors), and autistic children have been left notoriously unexploited, so that there is still some hope on this side. Should one conclude that it is time to return to common sense and pare down approaches to literary history? This is the thesis forcibly argued by Antoine Compagnon, a former disciple of Barthes who begins his elegant survey *The Demon of Theory* (or perhaps is it *The Imp of the Theoretical*)[8] by echoing the title of one of Kundera's first novels, *Laughable Loves.* He asks "What is left of our loves?" by which he refers to the past domination of High Theory. His conclusion is a rather conservative one, in the sense that he sees the main thrust of Theory as a subversion of common-sense ideas (for instance, the author is not the key to the meaning of the text, reference to the world out there is an illusion since what matters is the way language reflects itself, style is not a rational choice but an unconscious determination, and so on) and admits that on most issues the battle has been lost.

Compagnon scrutinizes a number of cruxes left by Theory like authorial intention, referentiality, the role of the reader, the function of style as a conscious choice; he tries to strike a neat balance between what can be saved of the onslaught on common sense wielded by structuralism and poststructuralism and what common sense believes. While I agree with most of these astute remarks about the need to revise concepts of literary criticism insofar as they deflate bombast and correct obvious exaggerations, I cannot help noticing that this problematic remains excessively literary and thus fails to touch upon the core of what I tend to understand by Theory. For instance, if we may agree that a measure of common sense will put an end to projective and philosophical over-interpretations of texts, will we have to return to the old humanism based on universal values our grandparents believed in? As the previous pages have demonstrated, Theory is as much concerned by the critique of ideologies as by close reading, as much invested in broad cultural issues as in the patient classification of literary processes. I felt the need then to produce my own "ideogram" of what I call Theory, and, true to my hystericization postulate, I felt compelled to descend to an *ad hominem* or *feminam* level, in short, to name people.

This is what led me to devise two lists. The first is the list of the key figures I have taught under the heading of Theory for the last century, imagining that I was allowed twenty names only, since condensation is the essence of pedagogy. Here, therefore, is my selection of canonical authors, without any concern for chronology or order. I found that these names tended to create couples either as accomplices or as dialoguing adversaries: Lacan–Kristeva; Benjamin–Adorno; Bakhtin–Barthes; Heidegger–Derrida; Foucault–Deleuze; Blanchot–De Man; Eagleton–Žižek; Levinas–Irigaray; Jameson–Bourdieu; Spivak–Said. Of course, I am aware that I have omitted important writers, but I provide this relatively standard roll-call with the wish of making more relevant another reduced list of relatively new authors. As a consequence, I had to shorten it – the century has only just begun after all – and list in alphabetical order just seven thinkers who all explore significantly different paths, who all master important areas of philosophy and evince a keen literary or artistic sense: Giorgio Agamben, Alain Badiou, Hans Blumenberg, Jean-Luc Nancy, Dorothea Olkowsky, Arkady Plotnisky, Peter Sloterdijk. Some are younger than others, and I take into account an Anglo-Saxon context in which certain philosophers take longer than others to be known or translated (this would be the case for Badiou for instance). Some introduce us to a more sweeping survey of an entire culture (Blumenberg and the thesis of the "readability of the world"), while others have a stronger focus or political affiliation (like Olkowsky as a feminist and a Deleuzian). They all refer often to the twenty "canonical" writers I have named while working each with a very distinctive and recognizable style.

An old joke goes like this: in theory, theory and practice are one; but in practice, they have nothing to with each other. This was the joke played upon Freud by Charcot, as we have seen. By dint of pondering what the old French master had meant, Freud ended up elaborating a global theory which culminated in a mythical creation looking back to Plato for sexuality and to Empedocles for the death instinct. Although there seems to be a general consensus about the schools which testify to the survival of Theory in the first decade of this century, in practice one needs to identify tasks, to select agendas, to point directly to names and faces. Thus, here again is a rather subjective listing of ten schools whose cumulative effort seems to map out Theory's main projects:

Conclusion

1 The New Arcades Projects, from Benjamin to new materialisms and new historicisms applied to various cultural landscapes: a history of material culture is still in the making with new privileged objects (clothes, hair, body parts, ornaments, excrements, monuments).

2 Technological criticism: the endlessly productive interactions between the human and machines, aesthetics of the technological sublime, virtual realities and possible worlds, Virilio's dromologies, Kittler's recording machines, the digital ticking linking cybers and ciphers.

3 Diasporic Criticism: migrations and literature, studies of displaced groups and emerging communities, with a focus on the notions of "home" (Rosemary George) and foreignness, leading to Globalization Studies assessing the transformations of the old nation-states and their literary versions, from transnationalisms (like new idioms and currencies in European Community politics or the dissemination of religions in post-colonial Africa) to returns to nationalism, with sites of resistance and new utopias.

4 Ethical criticism with a focus on revisions of sexual difference: from the ethics of otherness in sexuality, politics, and literature (Levinas, Lacan, Irigaray), to bioethical criticism in the context of post-humanism and to legal studies seeing not only the law as narrative but as a clash between the law and justice (Derrida), including issues of copyright and moral authority.

5 Testimonial Studies, taking trauma, genocide, and torture (Elaine Scary) as limit-points from which one may try to map collective histories, archives, or half-erased personal traces of unspeakable sufferings.

6 Genetic Criticism and new textual studies: from drafts, archives, editions (Jerome McGann and European Geneticists) to hypertextual studies, new research configurations generated by the critical hypertexts and interactive CD-Roms of canonical books; theories of the post-history of the book: what remains of the traditional institutions of literature (prizes, bookstores, email distribution centers) in the age of the e-book.

7 Science-and-Text Studies: literature and chaos theory, fractal

theory, catastrophe theory, complexity theory, Borromean knots, Lacanian mathemes, Gödelian theorems applied to literary formalization (Plotnisky, Vappereau).

8 "Hauntology" or Spectral Criticism (Wolfreys), pushing deconstruction closer to its religious limits, producing a clash between intertextuality and the "sacred," from the issue of the unspeakability of God's name to the question of returns to fundamentalisms as threats to literature's autonomy (Rushdie).

9 Hybridity studies: whiteness, yellowness, and blackness as constructs, color as projection of unconscious linguistic patterns, racism and the narcissism of small differences as reflected and deflected by literary studies, sociology, and psychoanalysis (Žižek).

10 Translation studies, from biblical studies to Antoine Berman's groundbreaking categories, moving from practical studies of cases to general definitions of style, language, intertextuality; the budding science or "techne" of traductology appears as a promising domain of investigation for literary theory.

Out of these broad schools several important agendas or special projects can be seen emerging. I will sketch six as particularly relevant to current interests in the field of Theory:

1 A renewed dialogue between Lacanian and Levinassian ethics in the context of a redefined "post-humanism."

2 Badiou's critique of historicism and assessment of Deleuze's philosophy away from purely "rhizomatic" anarchism, pointing to crucial interactions with science, film, and politics.

3 Rereadings of the Nietzsche–Heidegger confrontation in terms of current controversies over bioethics and the need for a new definition of the human (Sloterdijk).

4 A rethinking of technology as science and/or art, from Derridian points of view (Stiegler, Plotnisky, Beardsworth) or from the side of art criticism (Gilbert-Rolfe).

5 A much needed critical assessment of Blanchot's and Bataille's legacy leading to a reconsideration of the foundations of historical communities with the help of Nancy's and Agamben's insights.

6 A systematic confrontation between modes of Eastern and Western *logos*, from parallel assessments of the roles of Socrates and Confucius as rough contemporaries to issues of science and power in China (François Jullien), dialogue and authority in ancient Greece and China (G. E. R. Lloyd), with inroads into the links between Buddhist logic and mysticism in European philosophy.

Like the others, this list is by no means limitative; it aims more at stimulating the imagination than actually providing a repertory. Finally, I want to say how much there is to gain from constructive dialogues with trenchant but open adversaries of Theory like Stanley Cavell, Joseph Margolis, or William Gass – often the issue is not one of strategic affiliation or infeodation but of a choice of the right adversary.

Given the presence of so many philosophers in my ideal lists, I ought to stress once more the complex relationship between Theory and philosophy. We have seen how the impact of "continental" theorists (French, German, Italian, Russian) in the American universities has been to force English majors to read Plato, Aristotle, Kant, Hegel, Nietzsche, Husserl, or Heidegger, suddenly postulating familiarity with a new library not as a prerequisite in a curriculum but as a way of grappling with all sorts of "new" questions hiding very old problems. The hystericization effect I have described explains what kind of philosophy I mean: it is a philosophy for non-philosophers, a philosophy for those who want to walk on the streets without falling into a manhole, a philosophy for those who do not plan to be taken as professionals. First, life is too short, then often really interesting problems strike beginners with more clarity than jaded experts, and finally new issues tend to appear in the divides, hinges, margins of the domains. This movement goes beyond the opposition between logical positivism in the Anglo-Saxon mode and a continental respect for a tradition identified with the series of great names in the history of philosophy, or beyond the recurrent clash between those who want to start thinking here and now about linguistic, perceptual, or scientific problems and those who believe that one should begin by examining all the predecessors' discourses as they saturate any given field. For the hystericization of Theory insists upon its "now" and it does not offer any choice in the list of authors called upon – Wittgenstein will work as well as Heidegger, Peirce as well as Nietzsche. I am not just calling for a return to philosophy as a more stable site of discourse after all others have failed, but I am suggesting that Theory should work through philosophy relentlessly, destabilizing it in the name of other discourses, among which literature will only provide one strategy, and not a particularly privileged access.

One immediate danger is that this movement may lead to hasty or uninformed philosophizing; I shall restate that the aim of Theory is not to make students become specialists of this or that philosophy. On the other hand, as Badiou has insisted,[9] philosophy is not only possible but necessary; however, this necessity only appears when it distances itself from historicism. Here, therefore, is my central contention: Theory should go back to philosophy not as a history of philosophy or a philosophy of history, but as the systematic hystericization of philosophical problems. In fact, the model, in spite of all the anti-Platonic gestures multiplied by French or American theorists, would look back to Plato's Socrates, who loved nothing like wonder and seduction, and who, moreover, believed that any untaught slave or child could rediscover the principles of science provided the right questions were asked. I have dwelt at length only on some of these questions. These questions, once articulated together architectonically, will then build a problematic, that is a set of problems which may or may not be traditional, and will provide a discourse allowing one to mediate between the irreducible singularity of given texts (whatever their nature may be) and the generality of repeatable procedures of analysis underpinned by well-defined concepts. This is the moment that will ineluctably be present in any publishable text, not in the scholarly footnotes but in the opening pages or paragraphs where the first moves, the gambit, and the stakes appear, whether it belongs to literary studies or to cultural studies, and this is the crucial moment of justification for all these efforts, a moment that can be highlighted – and hopefully taught – by Theory.

Notes

Introduction

1 Quoted in *The Critical Tradition*, ed. David H. Richter (Boston and New York: Bedford and St. Martin's Press, 1998), p. 1514.

2 Ibid, p. 1515.

3 Friedrich Nietzsche, *Philosophy and Truth*, ed. and trans. Daniel Breazeale (Atlantic Highlands, NJ: Humanities Press International, 1991), p. 141.

4 Judith Butler, *Subjects of Desire* (New York: Columbia University Press, 1999).

5 Emily Eakins, "What Is the Next Big Idea? The Buzz is Growing," *New York Times, Arts & Ideas*, Saturday July 7, 2001, pp. B7, B9.

6 Michael Hardt and Antonio Negri, *Labor of Dionysus: A Critique of the State-Form* (Minneapolis: University of Minnesota Press, 1994).

7 Ibid, p. 3.

8 Michael Hardt and Antonio Negri, "What the Protesters in Genoa Want," *New York Times*, July 20, 2001, p. A21.

9 Ibid.

10 Michèle Lamont, "How to Become a Dominant French Philosopher: The Case of Jacques Derrida," *The American Journal of Sociology* (1987), quoted by Emily Eakins, "What Is the Next Big Idea?" p. B9.

11 Thomas Carlyle, *Sartor Resartus*, ed. Kerry McSweeney and Peter Sabor (Oxford: Oxford University Press, 1999), p. 22.

12 André Breton, *Oeuvres* vol. 1, ed. M. Bonnet, P. Bernier, E.-A. Hubert, and J. Pierre (Paris: Gallimard, Pléiade, 1988), p. 948. Note that the text is written in small capitals throughout. One will find

a good English translation of parts of this manifesto in Elisabeth Roudinesco, *Jacques Lacqn & Co: A History of Psychoanalysis in France, 1925–1985*, trans. Jeffrey Mehlman (Chicago: University of Chicago Press, 1990), pp. 6–7.

13 The same article praising *Empire* quotes Stanley Aronowitz as saying that "Literary Theory has been dead for 10 years" (ibid, p. B9). The remark comes from someone who has been used to the rapid turnover of "new" theories. Ten years without a new gadget seems a long time indeed for our short-term attention span, unless new interactive games are regularly released on the market, which is exactly how *Empire* has been packaged.

14 Breton, *Oeuvres* vol. 1, p. 950. My translation modifies slightly that of Mehlman.

15 Ibid, p. 949.

16 Camille Paglia, "Junk Bonds and Corporate Raiders," in *Sex, Art and American Culture* (New York: Random House, 1992), p. 241.

17 Ibid, p. 227.

18 Ibid, p. 228.

19 Ibid, p. 229.

20 Ibid, p. 220.

21 Ibid, p. 222.

22 Ibid, p. 218.

23 Ibid, p. 213.

24 I am alluding to the presentation of the four discourses in *Seminar XVII: L'Envers de la psychanalyse* (Paris: Seuil, 1991), p. 31. Useful discussions are provided by Marc Bracher in *Lacan, Discourse and Social Change: A Psychoanalytical Cultural Criticism* (Ithaca, NY: Cornell University Press, 1993), pp. 53–80 and Bruce Fink, "The Master Signifier and the Four Discourses," in *Key Concepts of Lacanian Psychoanalysis*, ed. Dany Nobus (New York: Other Press, 1998), pp. 29–47.

25 Lacan, *Seminar XVII*, p. 239.

26 Sigmund Freud, "Analysis Terminable and Interminable," in *Therapy and Technique*, ed. Philip Rieff (New York: Macmillan, 1963), p. 266.

27 Jacques Lacan, *Television*, ed. Joan Copjec, trans. Denis Hollier, Rosalind Krauss, and Annette Michelson (New York: Norton, 1990), p. 19.

28 Bruce Fink, *The Lacanian Subject: Between Language and Jouissance* (Princeton, NJ: Princeton University Press, 1995), p. 133.

29 See John D. Barrow, *Theories of Everything* (Oxford: Clarendon Press, 1991) and *Impossibility: The Limits of Science and the Science of Limits* (Oxford: Oxford University Press, 1998).

30 Slavoj Žižek, *Le Plus sublime des hystériques – Hegel passe* (Paris: Point Hors Ligne, 1988). The thesis of this book is more or less identical with the idea developed by Žižek in *The Sublime Object of Ideology* (London: Verso, 1989) that Hegel is not a pre-Marxist philosopher but the first and main "post-Marxist" thinker.

31 Lacan, *Seminar XVII* p. 38 (my translation).

1   Genealogy One: Hegel's Plague

1 See Vincent Descombes, *Modern French Philosophy*, trans. L. Scott-Fox and J. M. Harding (Cambridge: Cambridge University Press, 1980), pp. 9–54.

2 Michael Hardt, *Gilles Deleuze: An Apprenticeship in Philosophy* (Minneapolis: University of Minnesota Press, 1993), pp. ix–xv.

3 I refer to number 12/13 of *Cahiers Marxistes-Léninistes* edited by Althusserian students of the École Normale Supérieure (Paris, Maspéro, July–October 1966). It had reprinted Stalin's 1950 text on language and linguistics in which Stalin attacks the idea that language is a superstructure (pp. 26–42).

4 Descombes, *Modern French Philosophy*, p. 27.

5 Alexandre Kojève, *Introduction to the Reading of Hegel*, trans. James H. Nichols (New York: Basic Books, 1969), p. 32.

6 Ibid, p. 42.

7 Ibid, p. 47.

8 See Francis Fukuyama, *The End of History and the Last Man* (New York: Avon Books, 1992).

9 Kojève, *Introduction to the Reading of Hegel*, pp. 158–9.

10 See Jon Stewart, ed., *The Hegel Myths and Legends* (Evanston, IL: Northwestern University Press, 1996).

11 Georges Bataille, *The Bataille Reader*, ed. F. Botting and S. Wilson (Oxford: Blackwell, 1997), pp. 296–300.

12 Hegel's 1805 fragment is quoted by Bataille in "Hegel, Death and Sacrifice," *The Bataille Reader*, p. 279, from an essay on death in Hegel by Kojève not translated in the English version of *Introduction to the Reading of Hegel*. See Alexandre Kojève, *Introduction à la lecture de Hegel* (Paris: Gallimard, 1947), p. 575.

13 Louis Althusser, "Man, That night" in *Early Writings: The Spectre of Hegel*, trans. G. M. Goshgarian (London: Verso, 1997), p. 172.

14 Ibid, p. 171.

15 Jean Hyppolite, *Logic and Existence*, trans. Leonard Lawlor and Amit Sen (Albany: State University of New York Press, 1997).

16 Hyppolite, *Logic and Existence*, p. 187, translation modified.

17 Martin Heidegger, *Hegel's Phenomenology of Spirit*, trans. P. Emad and K. Maly (Bloomington: Indiana University Press, 1988).

18 Hyppolite, *Logic and Existence*, p. 42.

19 Gilles Deleuze, review of Jean Hyppolite's *Logic and Existence* quoted in *Logic and Existence*, p. 193.

20 Jacques Derrida, *Introduction to Edmund Husserl's Origin of Geometry*, trans. John P. Leavey Jr. (Lincoln: University of Nebraska Press, 1989), p. 67.

21 Jacques Derrida, "From Restricted to General Economy: A Hegelianism without Reserve," in *Writing and Difference*, trans. Alan Bass (Chicago: University of Chicago Press, 1978), p. 251.

22 Jacques Derrida, "Violence and Metaphysics" in *Writing and Difference*, p. 126.

23 Hyppolite, *Logic and Existence*, appendix, p. 195.

24 *La Part du feu* (Paris: Gallimard, 1949), p. 312.

25 Ibid, p. 295.

26 Jean-Paul Sartre, *L'Etre et le néant: essai d'ontologie phénoménologique* (Paris: Gallimard, 1943), p. 300.

27 Maurice Merleau-Ponty, *Notes de cours 1959–1961*, ed. Claude Lefort (Paris: Gallimard, 1996), p. 348.

28 Althusser, *Early Writings*, p. 171.

29 Richard Macksey and Eugenio Donato, eds., *The Languages of Criticism and the Sciences of Man: The Structuralist Controversy* (Baltimore: Johns Hopkins University Press, 1970) and Richard Macksey and Eugenio Donato, eds., *The Structuralist Controversy: The Languages of Criticism and the Sciences of Man* (Baltimore: Johns Hopkins University Press, 1972).

30 Macksey and Donato, *The Languages of Criticism and the Sciences of Man*, p. 168.

31 Ibid, p. 158.

32 Ibid, p. 314.

33 Quoted in Macksey and Donato, *The Structuralist Controversy*, "The Space Between – 1971," p. x.

34 Michel Foucault, *The Archeology of Knowledge*, trans. A. M. Sheridan Smith (New York: Pantheon, 1972), pp. 200–1.

35 Macksey and Donato, *The Structuralist Controversy*, "The Space Between – 1971," pp. x–xi.

36 Macksey and Donato, *The Languages of Criticism and the Sciences of Man*, p. 29.
37 Ibid, p. 29
38 Ibid, pp. 43–4.
39 Ibid, p. 121.
40 Ibid, p. 122.
41 Ibid, p. 121.
42 Ibid, p. 189.
43 Ibid, p. 188.
44 Ibid, p. 194.
45 Ibid, p. 150.
46 Ibid, p. 150.
47 Ibid, p. 184.
48 Ibid, p. 185.
49 Ibid, pp. 184–5.
50 Ibid, p. 155.
51 Ibid, pp. 155–6.
52 Ibid, pp. 146–7.
53 I have analyzed Althusser's changing assessment of Lacan and Derrida's critique of Lacan in my *Jacques Lacan* (London: Macmillan, 2001), pp. 19–20, 42–53.
54 Louis Althusser, "Letter to D." (July 18, 1966) in *Writings on Psychoanalysis: Freud and Lacan*, trans. Jeffrey Mehlman (New York: Columbia University Press, 1996), pp. 48–9.
55 Ibid, p. 51.

2   *Genealogy Two: The Avant-Garde at Theory's High Tide*

1 Sylvère Lotringer, "Doing Theory" in *French Theory in America*, ed. Sylvère Lotringer and Sande Cohen (New York: Routledge, 2001), p. 140.
2 Max Horkheimer, *Critical Theory: Selected Essays*, trans. Matthew K. O'Connell and others (New York: Continuum, 1995).
3 Max Horkheimer quotes Husserl's *Formal and Transcendental Logic* at the beginning of "Traditional and Critical Theory," *Critical Theory: Selected Essays*, p. 190.
4 Horkheimer, *Critical Theory: Selected Essays*, p. 221.
5 Ibid, p. 226.
6 Ibid, p. 233–4.

7   Ibid, p. 114–21.

8   Ibid, p. 123.

9   Jacques Lacan, "Les Complexes familiaux dans la formation de l' individu," in *Autres écrits*, ed. J. A. Miller (Paris: Seuil, 2001), p. 24. For a very thorough analysis of the contents of this essay, see Elisabeth Roudinesco, *Jacques Lacan & Co: A History of Psychoanalysis in France, 1925–1985*, trans. Jeffrey Mehlman (Chicago: University of Chicago Press, 1990), pp. 140–9.

10 Lacan, *Autres écrits*, p. 56.

11 Ibid, p. 60.

12 Ibid, p. 61.

13 Roudinesco, *Jacques Lacan*, p. 148.

14 Walter Benjamin, "The Concept of Criticism in German Romanticism" (1919) in *Selected Writings Volume 1, 1913–1926*, ed. Marcus Bullock and Michael W. Jennings (Cambridge, MA: Harvard University Press, 1996), p. 142.

15 Walter Benjamin's letter to Adorno (10/6/1938) in Theodor Adorno and Walter Benjamin, *The Complete Correspondence 1928–1940*, ed. Henri Lonitz, trans. Nicholas Walker (Cambridge, MA: Harvard University Press, 1999), p. 258.

16 Ibid, p. 259.

17 Walter Benjamin, *The Arcades Project*, trans. Howard Eiland and Kevin McLaughlin (Cambridge, MA: Harvard University Press, 1999), p. 460.

18 Adorno and Benjamin, *The Complete Correspondence 1928–1940*, p. 282.

19 Ibid, p. 283.

20 Ibid, p. 283.

21 Ibid, p. 284.

22 Ibid, p. 290.

23 Ibid, p. 283.

24 Ibid, p. 292.

25 See the excellent "Presentation" of the Adorno–Benjamin correspondence by Fredric Jameson in his editon of *Aesthetics and Politics* (Adorno, Benjamin, Bloch, Brecht, Lukács) (London: Verso, 1977), pp. 100–9.

26 Ibid, pp. 107–8.

27 T. W. Adorno, *Kierkegaard: Construction of the Aesthetic*, trans. Robert Hullot-Kentor (Minneapolis: University of Minnesota Press, 1989), p. 20.

28 Ibid, p. 41.

29 Ibid, p. 54.

30 Benjamin, *The Arcades Project*, p. 461.

31 J. M. Coetzee, "The Marvels of Walter Benjamin," *The New York Review of Books*, vol. 48, no. 1, January 11, 2001, p. 33.

32 Adorno and Benjamin, *The Complete Correspondence 1928–1940*, p. 290.

33 Coetzee, "The Marvels of Walter Benjamin," p. 33.

34 See Sigmund Freud's "Charcot" (1893) in *The Standard Edition of the Complete Psychological Works of Sigmund Freud*, general editor James Strachey, in collaboration with Anna Freud and others (London: Hogarth Press and the Institute of Psychoanalysis, 1974), vol. 3, p. 13. Also vol. 1, p. 139. For this point, see Malcolm Bowie, *Freud, Proust and Lacan: Theory as Fiction* (Cambridge: Cambridge University Press, 1987), pp. 14–15, 180.

35 Mikhail Bakhtin, *Toward a Philosophy of the Act*, ed. and trans. Vadim Liapunov and Michael Holquist (Austin: University of Texas Press, 1993), p. 40.

36 Ibid, p. 54.

37 Ibid, p. 55.

38 Ibid, p. 74.

39 Ibid, p. 75.

40 Ibid, p. 20.

41 For a useful account see Katerina Clark and Michael Holquist, *Mikhail Bakhtin* (Cambridge, MA: Harvard University Press, 1984), pp. 142–3.

42 Lynn Pearce, *Reading Dialogics* (London: Edward Arnold, 1994) and David Lodge, *After Bakhtin* (New York: Routledge, 1990).

43 See "The Heteroglot Novel" in *The Bakhtin Reader* ed. Pam Morris (London: Edward Arnold, 1994), pp. 94–6.

44 "The Problem of the Text in Linguistics, Philology and the Human Sciences: An Experiment in Philosophical Analysis," in Mikhail Bakhtin, *Speech Genres and Other Late Essays*, trans. Vern W. McGee, ed. Caryl Emerson and Michael Holquist (Austin: University of Texas Press, 1986), p. 116.

45 See, for instance, the very useful survey provided by Tiphaine Samoyault in *L'Intertextualité: mémoire de la littérature* (Paris: Nathan, 2001).

46 Roland Barthes, *Writing Degree Zero* (1953), trans. A. Lavers and C. Smith (New York: Noonday Press, 1968), p. 1.

47 Roland Barthes, *Le Degré zéro de l'écriture* (1953), in *Oeuvres Complètes, tome 1, (1942–1965)*, ed. Eric Marty (Paris: Seuil, 1993), p. 139.

48 Barthes, *Writing Degree Zero*, p. 1, footnote.

49 Roland Barthes, "What is Writing?" in *Writing Degree Zero*, pp. 10–11.

50 Barthes, *Writing Degree Zero,* pp. 14–15.

51 Among many places, one finds the statement in Barthes's *Writer Sollers*, trans. Philip Thody (Minneapolis: University of Minnesota Press, 1987), p. 42.

52 See Patrick Ffrench, *The Time of Theory: A History of Tel Quel (1950–1983)* (Oxford: Clarendon Press, 1995), pp. 28–30. Ffrench shows very well how Bataille was the acclaimed hero of the review and Blanchot the precursor whose name was erased. One reason adduced by Sollers is that Blanchot's thought was too Hegelian. See ibid, p. 29.

53 See Niilo Kauppi, *The Making of an Avant-Garde: Tel Quel* (Berlin: Mouton de Gruyter, 1994).

54 See Philippe Forest, *Histoire de Tel Quel* (Paris: Seuil, 1995) and Patrick Ffrench and Roland-François Lack, eds. and trans., *The Tel Quel Reader* (London: Routledge, 1998). Also Patrick Ffrench, ed., *From Tel Quel to L'Infini: The Avant-garde and After* (London: Parallax, 1998).

55 Paul Valéry, "Tel Quel" in *Oeuvres* vol. 2, ed. Jean Hytier (Paris: Gallimard, Pléiade, 1966), pp. 473–781

56 Paul Valéry, "L'Enseignement de la poétique au Collège de France," in *Oeuvres* vol. 1, ed. Jean Hytier (Paris: Gallimard, Pléiade, 1965), p. 1438.

57 Ibid, p. 1440.

58 Ibid, p. 1441.

59 Valéry, *Oeuvres* vol. 2, p. 550.

60 Valéry, *Oeuvres* vol. 1, p. 1442; *Oeuvres* vol. 2, p. 478.

61 *Tel Quel* no. 1, Paris, March 1960, p. 1. For a relatively different translation see Niilo Kauppi's *The Making of an Avant-Garde,* p. 25.

62 Georges Bataille, "On Nietzsche: The Will to Chance" (1949), in *The Bataille Reader,* ed. F. Botting and S. Wilson (Oxford: Blackwell, 1997), p. 341.

63 See Kristin Ross's compelling analysis of French culture in the 1950s and 1960s, with special emphasis on the general fascination for "fast cars": *Fast Cars, Clean Bodies: Decolonization and the Reordering of French Culture* (Cambridge, MA: MIT Press, 1995), p. 27.

64 See Jacques Derrida, *Dissemination*, trans. Barbara Johnson (Chicago: University of Chicago Press, 1991), pp. 173–286, 289–366.

65 *Tel Quel: Théorie d'ensemble* (Paris: Seuil, 1968), p. 7.

66 "Division of the Assembly" in Ffrench and Lack, *The Tel Quel Reader*, pp. 22–3.
67 Ibid, p. 23.
68 Ffrench, *The Time of Theory*, p. 1.
69 See Michael Riffaterre, "Le Formalisme français," in *Essais de stylistique structurale* (Paris: Flammarion, 1971), p. 277. For a detailed and technical refutation, see pp. 269–284.
70 Jacques Roubaud and Philippe Lusson, "Sur la 'sémiologie des paragrammes' de Julia Kristeva," in *Action Poétique* nos. 41–2, 1969, pp. 56–61 and no. 45, 1970, pp. 31–6.
71 Philippe Sollers, *Women*, trans. Barbara Bray (New York: Columbia University Press, 1990), p. 320.
72 Julia Kristeva, "Brouillon d'inconscient ou l'inconscient brouillé," *Genesis* no. 8, special issue on manuscripts and psychoanalysis (Paris: CNRS, 1995), p. 24.

3 Theory, Science, Technology

1 Roland Barthes, *Mythologies*, selected and trans. Annette Lavers (New York: Noonday Press, 1972), p. 134.
2 Barthes, *Mythologies*, p. 126, footnote 7.
3 Roland Barthes, *Roland Barthes*, trans. Richard Howard (Berkeley: University of California Press, 1977), p. 71, slightly modified.
4 Roland Barthes, *The Pleasure of the Text*, trans. Richard Miller (New York: Hill and Wang, 1975), p. 26.
5 Jacques Derrida, "Deconstructions: The Im-possible" in *French Theory in America*, ed. Sylvère Lotringer and Sande Cohen (New York: Routledge, 2001), p. 19.
6 Ibid.
7 One anecdote can illustrate this. Richard Sieburth, Professor of French and Comparative Literature at NYU, told me that he had heard Brazilian students stopping a speaker in a special research seminar on literature. They wanted something different, they said; they wanted no literature, just "hard" Theory, because they had no time or leisure, they just needed "power tools" and could dispense with raw material. Theory only would provide the instruments they could then bring back home and apply to other contexts.
8 Geoffrey Bennington and Jacques Derrida, *Jacques Derrida* (Chicago: University of Chicago Press, 1991), p. 1.

9   Plato, *Protagoras*, trans. and annotated by C. C. W. Taylor (Oxford: Clarendon Press, 1991), p. 31. I will henceforth allude to this edition, while using the traditional pagination.

10   As Oded Balaban assumes, when he curiously equates Protagoras's hermeneutics with either Formalism or idle critical discussions of critics discussing other critics. See his *Plato and Protagoras: Truth and Relativism in Ancient Greek Philosophy* (Lanham, MD: Lexington Books, 1999), p. 231.

11   See Jacques Derrida, "Plato's Pharmacy" (1968) in *Dissemination*, trans. Barbara Johnson (Chicago: University of Chicago Press, 1982).

12   Joseph Margolis, *The Truth about Relativism* (Oxford: Blackwell, 1991), p. 147. The phrase quoted comes from *Of Grammatology*, p. 4.

13   See Michael Riffaterre, *Fictional Truth* (Baltimore, MD: Johns Hopkins University Press, 1990).

14   See Martin Heidegger, "The Question Concerning Technology" in *The Question Concerning Technology and other Essays*, trans. William Lovitt (New York: Harper and Row, 1977), pp. 19–24.

15   Ibid, p. 16.

16   Ibid, p. 18.

17   Ibid, p. 34.

18   Martin Heidegger, "Hölderlin and the Essence of Poetry" in *Elucidations of Hölderlin's Poetry*, trans. Keith Hoeller (Amherst, MA: Humanity Books, 2000), p. 61.

19   Martin Heidegger, *Erläuterungen zu Hölderlins Dichtung* (Frankfurt: Vittorio Klostermann, 1981), p. 45.

20   Martin Heidegger, "Science and Reflection" in *The Question Concerning Technology and other Essays*, p. 163.

21   For a very comprehensive development on this topic, see William McNeill, *The Glance of the Eye: Heidegger, Aristotle and the Ends of Theory* (Albany: State University of New York Press, 1999).

22   Heidegger, "Science and Reflection," p. 164.

23   Ibid, p. 165.

24   Hannelore Rausch, *Theoria: Von ihrer sakralen zur philosophischen Bedeutung* (Munich: Wilhelm Fink, 1982).

25   Heidegger, *Elucidations of Hölderlin's Poetry*, p. 64.

26   Hans Blumenberg, *Das Lachen der Thrakerin: Eine Urgeschichte der Theorie* (Frankfurt: Suhrkamp, 1987), p. 9.

27   Friedrich Nietzsche, *Philosophy and Truth: Selections from Nietzsche's Notebooks of the Early 1870s*, ed. and trans. Daniel Breazeale (Atlantic Highlands, NJ: Humanities Press, 1991), p. 33.

28   Ibid, p. 33.

4   Theory Not of Literature But as Literature

1   Roland Barthes, *Roland Barthes*, trans. Richard Howard (Berkeley: University of California Press, 1977), pp. 118–19.
2   Marcel Proust, *Time Regained* in *In Search of Lost Time* vol. 6, trans. Andreas Mayor and Terence Kilmartin, revd. D. J. Enright (New York: The Modern Library, 1999), pp. 278–9.
3   See Malcolm Bowie, *Freud, Proust and Lacan: Theory as Fiction* (Cambridge: Cambridge University Press, 1987), pp. 45–65.
4   See *Ulysses*, revd. edn. by H. W. Gabler (New York: Garland, 1986), U. 8:20 and U. 8:154.
5   Sigmund Freud, "On the Sexual Theories of Children," in *The Sexual Enlightenment of Children*, ed. Philip Rieff (New York: Collier Books, 1963), p. 28.
6   Samuel Beckett, *The Unnamable* in *Three Novels* (New York: Grove Press, 1991), p. 324.
7   Samuel Beckett, *Proust and Three Dialogues* (London: John Calder, 1970), p. 87.
8   Proust, *Time Regained*, p. 225.
9   James Joyce, *Finnegans Wake* (London: Faber, 1939), p. 8, l. 5.
10 James Joyce, *Selected Letters*, ed. Richard Ellmann (London: Faber, 1975), p. 19.
11 James Joyce, *Stephen Hero* (London: Jonathan Cape, 1956), p. 216.
12 Ibid, pp. 210–11.
13 James Joyce, *Ulysses*, U. 3:143.
14 Joyce, *Stephen Hero*, p. 216.
15 Ibid, pp. 216–17.
16 Ibid, p. 218.
17 Stanislaus Joyce, *My Brother's Keeper* (New York: Viking, 1958), pp. 134–5.
18 James Joyce, *Critical Writings*, ed. Ellsworth Mason and Richard Ellmann (New York: Viking, 1964), p. 145
19 Ibid, p. 46.
20 Arthur Power, *Conversations with James Joyce* (London: Millington, 1974), p. 36.
21 Samuel Henry Butcher, *Aristotle's Theory of Poetry and the Fine Arts* (London: Macmillan, 1895), p. 123.
22 See Jacques Aubert, *The Aesthetics of James Joyce* (Baltimore, MD: Johns Hopkins University Press, 1992) and R. J. Schork, *Greek and Hellenic Culture in Joyce* (Gainesville: University Press of Florida, 1998).

23 Butcher, *Aristotle's Theory of Poetry and the Fine Arts*, p. 153.

24 James Joyce, *A Portait of the Artist as a Young Man*, ed. C. Anderson (New York: Viking, 1968), p. 208.

25 See Ginette Verstraete, *Fragments of the Feminine Sublime in Friedrich Schlegel and James Joyce* (Albany: State University of New York Press, 1998).

26 Joyce, *Ulysses*, 15: 109.

27 See Paul de Man, "The Rhetoric of Blindness: Jacques Derrida's Reading of Rousseau," in *Blindness and Insight*, 2nd. edn. (London: Routledge, 1983), pp. 102–41. See also the very helpful guide by Martin McQuillan, *Paul de Man* (London: Routledge, 2001), pp. 21–9.

28 Milan Kundera, *The Art of the Novel*, trans. Linda Asher (New York: Grove Press, 1988).

29 Hermann Broch, *The Sleepwalkers*, trans. Willa and Edwin Muir (New York: Random House, 1996).

30 Plato, *Theaetetus*, trans. F. M. Cornford in *The Collected Dialogues* (Princeton, NJ: Princeton University Press, 1973), p. 879.

31 Hans Blumenberg, *Das Lachen der Thrakerin: Eine Urgeschichte der Theorie* (Frankfurt: Suhrkamp, 1987).

32 Honoré de Balzac, *Théorie de la démarche et autres textes* (Paris: Albin Michel, 1990), p. 27.

33 Proust had perfectly identified this streak in Balzac when he made fun of the scientific "physiognomies" in the opening of his excellent Balzac pastiche (but Balzac is the first of the authors he pastiches): "Only a physicist of the moral world who would have both Lavoisier's genius and Bichat's – the creator of organic chemistry – skills would be in measure to isolate the elements that compose the special sound of steps produced by superior men." Marcel Proust, *Contre Sainte-Beuve et pastiches et mélanges* (Paris: Gallimard,, Pléiade, 1971), p. 8.

34 G. W. F. Hegel, *The Phenomenology of Spirit,* trans. A. V. Miller (Oxford: Oxford University Press, 1977), p. 210.

35 Broch, *The Sleepwalkers*, p. 9.

36 Ibid, p. 10.

Conclusion

1 W. H. Auden, *The English Auden*, ed. Edward Mendelson (London: Faber; 1986), p. 81.

2 The best place to start in English is the lucid assessment provided by the special issue on "Drafts" of the *Yale French Studies* (no. 89, 1996). I have already quoted the lushly produced review called *Genesis* (Paris: J. M. Place) which regularly publishes archival files and interpretive essays.

3 Roland Barthes, *Writing Degree Zero*, trans. A. Lavers and C. Smith (New York: Noonday Press, 1968), p. 17.

4 See, for instance, Catherine Fuchs, Almuth Grésillon, Jean-Louis Lebrave, Jean Peytard, Josette Rey-Debove, and Antoine Culioli, *La Genèse du texte: les modèles linguistiques* (Paris: CNRS, 1982).

5 See Alan Sokal and Jean Bricmont, *Fashionable Nonsense: Postmodern Intellectuals' Abuse of Science* (New York: Picador, 1998), pp. 166–8.

6 See once more Derrida's "Structure, Sign and Play," in *Writing and Difference*, trans. Alan Bass (Chicago: University of Chicago Press, 1978), pp. 278–93.

7 Mark Shell, *Children of the Earth: Literature, Politics and Nationhood* (New York: Oxford University Press, 1993).

8 Antoine Compagnon, *Le Démon de la théorie* (Paris: Seuil, 1998).

9 See Alain Badiou's *Manifesto for Philosophy*, trans. and ed. Norman Madars (Albany: State University of New York Press, 1999).

Index